PATHS OF LIFE

ALSO BY ALICE MILLER

The Drama of the Gifted Child: The Search for the True Self

For Your Own Good: The Roots of Violence in Child-rearing

Thou Shalt Not Be Aware: Society's Betrayal of the Child

Pictures of a Childhood: Sixty-six Watercolors and an Essay

*The Untouched Key: Tracing Childhood Trauma
in Creativity and Destructiveness*

Banished Knowledge: Facing Childhood Injuries

*Breaking Down the Wall of Silence:
The Liberating Experience of Painful Truth*

*The Truth Will Set You Free:
Overcoming Emotional Blindness and Finding Your True Adult Self*

The Body Never Lies: The Lingering Effects of Cruel Parenting

REVISED AND UPDATED
10TH ANNIVERSARY EDITION

Alice Miller

PATHS OF LIFE

SIX CASE HISTORIES

*Translated by
Andrew Jenkins*

BASIC
BOOKS

A Member of the Perseus Books Group
NEW YORK

Previously published in 1999 by Vintage Books,
a division of Random House.

Originally published in Germany as *Wege des Lebens*
by Suhrkamp Verlag, Frankfort am Main.
Copyright © 1998 by Suhrkamp Verlag Frankfort am Main.
This translation originally published in hardcover in the
United States by Pantheon Books, a division of
Random House, Inc., New York, in 1998.

Author photograph © Julika Miller/Suhrkamp

Books published by Basic Books are available at
special discounts for bulk purchases in the United States
by corporations, institutions, and other organizations.
For more information, please contact the Special
Markets Department at the Perseus Books Group,
2300 Chestnut Street, Suite 200, Philadelphia, PA
19103, or call (800) 810-4145, ext. 5000, or
e-mail special.markets@perseusbooks.com.

A CIP catalog record for this book is available
from the Library of Congress.
ISBN: 978-0-465-01268-8
10 9 8 7 6 5 4 3 2 1

Contents

Preface   vii

SIX CASE HISTORIES

Claudia and Daniel: *Thirty Years Later*   3

Yolanta and Linda: *Really Welcome*   23

Anika: *Worth a Try*   38

Helga: *Trading on Tears*   50

Gloria: *Wisdom from the Heart*   79

Margot and Lilka: *Warsaw to Sydney and Back*   96

REFLECTIONS

Gurus and Cult Leaders: *How They Function*   123

What Is Hatred?   129

Afterword   159

Postscript   163

Notes   167

Preface

MOST PEOPLE are born into a family. This family will mark them for life. Critical as young people may be of their parents, sometimes to the extent of breaking with them altogether, there is no way of escaping the more or less indelible imprint that these first family influences leave. Awareness of this fact becomes inescapable when we have children of our own.

Many people give the matter little thought. They simply put their own children through the same things they experienced themselves when they were young, and they feel they are quite right to do so. But one day they find to their amazement and dismay that it is precisely with their children and spouses or companions that they have the toughest time achieving the inner freedom they have been striving for since their youth. They are then quite likely to feel that they have reached an impasse. As they found no way out of that impasse when they were children, they had no alternative but to knuckle under, to grin and bear it. And for some adults it seems to be just the same.

But it is not. For however much we may be the product of family background, of heredity, of upbringing (for better or for worse), as adults we can gradually learn to recognize these influences. Then we are no longer under the compulsion to behave like robots. The greater our awareness of the way we have been conditioned, the more likely we are to free ourselves from our entrapments and be receptive to new information.

The reader will become acquainted with a number of personal stories in the following pages. One of the things they are designed to illustrate is that the traces left by our childhood accompany us not only in the families of our own we have as adults, they manifest themselves in the very fabric of human society, all the way up to those outsize personalities who (again, for better or for worse) have left their imprint on the course of history. In my closing reflections, I turn to the question of whether and how we can learn to gain a clearer understanding of the way hatred evolves and thus prevent it from taking root.

As every life is unique, people naturally differ in the way they integrate their childhood into their adult lives. But regardless of the way individuals may decide to go, sensitivity to the harm done by a cruel childhood is increasing and that can only be a boon for society as a whole. Child abuse in all its forms has always been with us and it is still widespread today. But only recently have the victims started realizing what has been done to them and talking to other people about it. Subjects rarely touched on before are moving into the foreground of discussion, a discussion which opens up new perspectives of greater fulfillment in life for very many people.

This was brought home to me forcibly by a book I read recently.[1] In it, fourteen fathers serving prison sentences for sexual abuse of their children and taking part in a carefully structured group therapy designed during their term of imprisonment tell the story of their crimes. It is encouraging to see how the mentalities of these men changed after they were given the opportunity to talk about what they had been through and thus felt understood and accepted. As was to be expected, they are without exception stories of horrible deprivations in childhood, scenarios full of sexual exploitation masquerading as a substitute for the love they were denied.

When I say encouraging, I am referring to the transformation undergone by these men on the basis of the counseling and guidance they were given. They had lived thirty, forty, fifty years without ever being given the opportunity to scrutinize and investigate what they had been through as children, much less identify it as a wrong that had been done to them. Compulsively and without qualms, they inflicted the same suffering on their own children as they had been subjected to themselves. As long as they had no grasp of the way these things related to each other, they were unable to free themselves from that compulsion. Only now are they ready and willing to acknowledge their responsibility, because they no longer regard what happened to them in early youth as just the way things happen to be but have learned to see it as an outrageous wrong inflicted on them. Armed with this knowledge they can now mourn that horrible, twisted mess in their early lives where their childhood should have been.

This apprenticeship in critical thinking has not driven them into self-pity. Quite the contrary. From their own sufferings they have learned to empathize with their children and to acknowledge that they have harmed them for the rest of their lives. They are doing their best to repair that damage, but they know that much of it is irreversible. Not all of them have already succeeded in freeing themselves from this impasse. Some still have a long and difficult process ahead of them.

The figures in this book are my own inventions though not the stories themselves, which have accompanied me for a long time. In the course of writing, however, they developed a life and a set of dynamics of their own, which in its turn enabled me to expand on what I had learned over the last few years and give it a more graphic form. The persons described here are not intended as ideals to be emulated. They simply recount what has happened to them and how they have either succeeded or failed in coming to terms with it. In describing their destinies and their environments, I consciously decided to keep outward detail to a minimum and to concentrate on the relations between the figures, on their feelings and thoughts.

There is no ready-made recipe for liberating oneself from the consequences of early injuries. The objectives we have and the capacity for realizing them vary from person to person. Even if we are not able to live up to our full potential in childhood, and though the traces of earlier fears, uncertainties, and deprivations stay with us in our later lives, there is still much that we can do to change things for the better because our awareness has become more acute. This new awareness is frequently a result of encounters with feeling individuals who have been lucky enough to grow up surrounded by love and respect, who have had a less troubled childhood, who have experienced pleasure and freedom and have thus been able to lead easier, happier lives.

The figures most closely matching that description in my stories are probably Daniel, Michelle, Margot, Louise, perhaps even Gloria. They are able to listen, to identify with others; they are outgoing, concerned, and usually less prone to illusions than the figures we see them encountering. As they have experienced honesty and unconditional affection in their early years, they are better able to cope with their lives than those who are fed on illusions and later have to fight to find out the truth about themselves, like Claudia, Anika, Helga, or Lilka.

The informal, associative style of the book should not blind the reader to the fact that my intentions in writing it go beyond the issues involved in the individual biographies of these characters and seek to pose a number of more universal questions, most notably: How do early experiences of suffering and love affect people's later lives and the way they relate to others? There are modern branches of research into areas that would be part and parcel of any attempt to answer that question, for example, observation of life in the uterus, study of newborn babies and infants, the early lives of political dictators, statistics on genocide, and so forth. But as far as I know, research has yet to be done into the way the data already collected relate to the childhood experiences of the people actively involved. These stories and reflections are designed to provide a stimulus for organized inquiries in that direction.

SIX CASE HISTORIES

CLAUDIA AND DANIEL

Thirty Years Later

CLAUDIA AND DANIEL WERE fellow students at Berkeley in the sixties. They were also lovers. Among the other students, Claudia had the reputation of being a "good listener," but also of keeping herself very much to herself. In their physical relationship, Daniel experienced her as warm-hearted and giving, but he also sensed a kind of deep-seated mistrust, a fearful reticence. She seemed to be longing for frank, uncomplicated intimacy, but at the same time she displayed an obvious reluctance to let herself go. It was as if she were shielding herself from something, but he did not know what it was. One day she announced out of the blue that she was getting married—to Max. Max? Daniel could hardly imagine two people with less in common than Claudia and Max.

Later Daniel got married himself. It was an unhappy marriage. But after the divorce he met Monica, and with her he was able to have the kind of relationship he had always hoped for.

Recently at a conference in San Diego (both of them are now psychotherapists), Claudia and Daniel met again. They had not been in touch for thirty years, so they were doubly glad to meet up after all this time.

Daniel has not changed much; but Claudia, the timid Berkeley student, is now a mature woman. The old rapport is still there, and soon they are telling each other about the way things have gone for them.

"You know," Daniel says, "I could never understand how you came to marry Max of all people. Whenever you crossed my mind in these last thirty years, I ended up thinking maybe you purposely opted to live with a man you didn't love and who was so different from you, because that way you couldn't get hurt. We never talked about that kind of thing when we were at Berkeley, do you remember? I wish you'd tell me something about your childhood. After all, I knew Max too."

"I'm glad you asked," Claudia answers spontaneously. "I really did love you, you know, and for a long time I had this dream of telling you everything. But it's a long story, so if you don't mind I'll write to you instead."

Two weeks later, Daniel gets a long letter.

Dear Daniel,

Spurred on by your interest, I'm taking the opportunity (not for the first time!) to look back on my marriage and try to take stock. I'm sitting in my garden, which I love, and I'm hoping that I can face up to the memories I'll be putting down on paper.

In retrospect, I see my marriage as one long, futile struggle, basically as a torment. I did all I could to get close to my husband. He claimed that he loved me, he was never unfaithful, he was never violent, he was a good provider. But the last thing he wanted was any kind of intimacy, with me or any other woman. He kept his feelings and his own past hidden from himself and from me. Just like I did, only much more so. And yet behind that front I sensed a longing for warmth, and I hoped one day I might be able to satisfy that longing.

So the goal I set myself, as a kind of "full-time job," was to break down the walls my husband had put up around himself, to penetrate to the core of his being and to communicate with him. But the whole undertaking was doomed from the outset. Max didn't want to open up; he just wanted to be "left in peace," as he put it. He was a typical "rationalist," quite happy to communicate with me on a purely conventional basis. The only time he showed any signs of having an emotional life at all was during love-making or when he got angry. Anything going beyond that was suspect, alien, dangerous, something either to be pitied or made fun of. I guessed that the reason he was so closed-off must have something to do with his childhood, a conclusion I came to from the rare occasions when he made any reference to his youth. It was a long time before I got to know the details.

In my purse I had a photo of him that was taken when he was three. Whenever he had hurt me, I took it out and looked at it. It stopped me from feeling resentful. Resentment wasn't what I wanted. What I wanted was to understand him. I felt an immense sympathy for that little boy with the cute face and the quizzical expression. I only had to look at that picture and all my hurt was forgotten. No more pain, no more anger. That way I was always willing to forgive the adult man that child in the photo had turned into. But ultimately I was harming myself. The greater my attachment to the child in him, the more I lost sight of myself and the position I was in, and the more obvious his rejection of me became. The last thing he wanted was to let that child live, to have any lingering intimations of what he had once been. I imagine he felt threatened by my attempts to get close to him; the protective wall got higher and higher all the time.

They say opposites attract. Is that why I married Max? I honestly think the differences were less apparent when we first met. At that time I too was afraid of my own feelings; I too was hiding from myself. But even in intellectual discussions, we never really spoke the same language. We were on two different planets.

There are lots of things that can cement a relationship: sex, children, a home, going away together. But if it all just serves to cover up a fundamental disconnection, it's no good trying to paper over the cracks. In the end they always show through: illnesses, unnecessary surgery, things like that. It's what happened to me, anyway.

It was an awful struggle before I finally admitted to myself that I wanted a divorce. Max was dead set against it; he insisted he couldn't carry on without me. I was on the verge of a breakdown; I believed him when he said that and I felt responsible for the way his life would turn out. On the other hand, I didn't want to pay for his life with my own. But no sooner were we divorced than Max found himself a new wife and seemed to get along with her just fine. So I stopped feeling guilty. Luckily there are women whose needs are different from mine. With a woman like that, Max maybe didn't feel so defensive. With her he could finally cultivate his nicer sides and achieve his ideal of a secure middle-class home without what he called "all that agonizing."

At first I tried to give him that kind of home, although it meant denying my true self. Early on, I had had the experience of being made to feel inadequate as a person, and for a long time I was unable to put up any resistance. I always had to be on hand for my parents, always available for whatever it was they needed me for. My father was an alcoholic. He could be very winning at times, but he was just as liable to fly off the handle for no apparent reason. My mother had cancer and had to go to the hospital on a number of occasions. Sometimes I went to see her there with my father. Of course I was sorry for them; they were so unhappy. I wanted to do all I could to help them. But as a child there was nothing I could do. That combination of extreme helplessness and an overgrown sense of responsibility for others left a lasting imprint on my later life. It took me ages to give it up.

As an only child, I felt lonely and I desperately sought contact with my parents; I would have done anything they asked if I could have felt really close to them. But it was all in vain. There were times when they were nice to me, but then for no reason I could fathom, my father would suddenly crumple and crawl back to the liquor bottle again, putting up an impenetrable wall, cutting himself off from me and the things I wanted to ask him. And most of the time my mother was way out of earshot, too, preoccupied with an illness which as a child I never really understood but which somehow made me feel guilty.

I did what I could to not feel anything—no resentment, no sorrow, no anger. But I can still remember the feeling of longing. It sometimes caught me by the throat when I heard the trains hooting in the distance. It was a mixture of deep sadness and a desire to escape, to get away from the constant loneliness, the endless feeling of not being able to cope. I dreamed of far-away lands where people were nice to one another, people you could rely on.

Then I fell in love with you. I never felt responsible for the kind of shape you happened to be in. You were so different from my parents; we could talk about anything and everything. I felt connected with you. The things I'd been looking for suddenly seemed so near; I would have so loved to stay with you. But I just couldn't trust my luck, I wasn't used to it; I was afraid of disappointing you, afraid you might leave me. So I started fighting that desire to stay with you, fighting the feelings I had for you, so that I would never have to suffer as I had in my childhood. It was all I knew. What I didn't know was that it doesn't always have to be that way. So I went on torturing myself.

I expect my decision to marry Max must have come as a big surprise to you. After all, he stood for everything I disliked. He was cagey, hidebound, interested only in abstract problems, very conventional. He knew better about everything, and he was a rotten listener. I didn't see it so clearly at the time, of course. But I did sense it. So what made me marry a man like that?

I thought, okay, he's pigheaded, but that's his strength; he won't start drinking whatever happens, so he won't leave me either. This conviction, unrealistic as it was, made me feel safe. My father's unreliability and unpredictability had always scared me. Whenever something was preying on his mind, he grabbed for the bottle. He immersed himself in booze and that put him right out of my reach. He never gave me any explanation, any information that would have helped me understand him.

Sometimes the liquor had the effect of putting him in a towering rage, and I racked my brains for what I might have done to provoke his anger. Whenever mother was hospitalized, I was left alone with him and his moods, and it was sheer hell. That's what made me look out for a "steady" husband, someone to lean on. But you displayed your feelings; you were vulnerable. And that made me afraid of my love for you, afraid it might plunge me into the same abyss as my love for my father did. I was afraid the day might come when I couldn't reach you, either.

In Max I thought I had found the opposite of my father, a rock that I might hurt myself on but one I could hide behind as well. But looking back I now see that the things that made me suffer during my marriage were basically the same things I had hated when I was still living at home. Max didn't drink; he was always sober. Yet his way of making himself scarce, inaccessible was even more foolproof than liquor. He had used his intellect to put up such impenetrable walls around his feelings that he wasn't capable of any kind of genuine communication at all, not even in exceptional situations. All I got from him was criticism, blame, scathing remarks, at best ironical jibes. Just saying something nice, without lacing it with sarcasm, was something completely foreign to him.

So marrying Max left me in the same kind of isolation I had experienced with my parents. It must sound absurd for an outsider, but in all seriousness I was expecting Max of all people to give me something that he was least equipped to provide: open, warm-hearted communication. I was unflagging in my attempts to reach him and wasn't going to give up hope that easily. But as I never had that kind of experience in my own childhood, I was unable to see that such openness between us might in fact be completely impossible.

Only years later did I realize that I had a choice. I didn't have to sacrifice myself; there was no point waiting for someone

to change who had no intention of changing because he had
never questioned his own opinions. Today I enjoy being able to
really talk with people, my husband, Mark, above all, and some
good friends.

Unfortunately, the divorce was not the end of the story of
my marriage. It repeated itself in my relationship with my oldest
daughter Carla. With her I kept on relapsing into that old childhood pattern, those constant feelings of inadequacy, guilt, helplessness. Luckily I have managed to establish an affectionate
relationship with my two younger daughters. With them I feel
relatively free. And I know of many cases where very close contact with the children has been possible despite divorce.

But between Carla and me there was such a yawning chasm
that whatever I did I couldn't seem to bridge it. For a long time
I put it down to repressed experiences from my own childhood,
ill-defined but tormenting anxieties that pervaded my entire
body during and after Carla's birth. It's not surprising that it
should have put a strain on our relationship from the outset. I
believe that Carla's initial disorientation and uncertainty left its
mark on her until well into adult life. Also, of my daughters she
was the one who suffered most from the breakdown of our
marriage. I was looking to that child to rescue me from the
nonrelationship my marriage represented. And what newborn
child can live up to that kind of expectation? As so often
happens, her fate was sealed well before her birth.

When I was expecting Carla, I attended a class where you
learn how to change and feed your baby. These preparations
were the basis for a kind of dialogue with Carla, albeit a silent
one. I often used to walk the whole distance to class, immersed
in silent conversation with my baby. That way I could free
myself to some extent from the almost permanent anguish I was
living in. Today I can say that I was really looking forward to the

birth, but the way a prisoner looks forward to freedom, a freedom I hoped would fulfill my longings for a genuine relationship. I wasn't looking forward to it like a woman ready and
willing to welcome a new baby and attend to what this little
creature needs. I was starving for love, but I wasn't mature and
fulfilled enough to be able to give any genuine love and affection myself.

When Carla was born, I really didn't have the faintest idea
what goes on inside the head of a newborn baby. I just gave
myself over to the ministrations of the trained staff at the hospital and went along with everything they said, like a good,
nicely brought-up girl who doesn't want to cause anyone any
trouble. My body tried to make itself heard but, unfortunately,
in the form of symptoms that put me at the mercy of the
nursing staff.

Soon I was producing too much milk and had a breast infection. The condition was treated with camphor and quickly
cleared up. But from then on the baby refused to breast-feed;
she cried and protested all the time. Today, I know that camphor
functions by reducing lactation and that in its turn gets rid of
the infection quicker. What I didn't know at the time was that
after this kind of treatment breast-feeding is experienced by
mother and child as something negative, if it is possible at all.
These days they've stopped that particular camphor treatment.

It was only a few years ago that I finally understood what
happened in that hospital twenty-eight years back. I chanced on
a book by Françoise Dolto, a French child psychiatrist, in which
she says that the very first thing a newborn baby uses for orien-
tation purposes is the smell of the mother.[1] This familiar smell is
what helps the baby to recognize the mother immediately after
birth and to salvage the feelings of safety and security experienced in the womb and preserve them in the new surroundings.

In French, the word for this recognition is *reconnaissance,* which also means "gratitude." How can a woman smelling of camphor communicate to a newborn child that she is the mother, that she has the best of intentions, has enough milk, and is eager to breast-feed her baby? A baby will trust his senses. And if the smell is alien and offputting, this is the child's reality and there's nothing anyone can do about it.

I imagine that the child's reaction is something like this: "I came out into this strange world after a long, scary birth and you didn't take me into your sheltering arms; you didn't console me. You let them take me away and didn't give me the reassuring skin contact I needed. You betrayed me. How can I ever trust you again? I'm in constant fear of being so terribly disappointed all over again." It may be that Carla's deep-seated distrust of me has to do with that early experience. The other reasons that came later were then the logical consequences of a relationship that was already badly undermined.

I was so unsure of myself in those first few days that I thought my baby would be better off and happier in other people's care. It was before the positive experiences I had with my other daughters, and I had absolutely no confidence in myself as a mother whatever. So on many occasions I left Carla in the care of the people who worked for us. That was bound to make her feel rejected because in spite of her mistrust, she was still looking for her mother.

Today I believe that if at Carla's birth someone had encouraged me to express my fears, that would have enabled me to better understand the distress my child was in. The relationship between Carla and me would probably not have been so traumatic and I wouldn't have had to go in search of surrogate mothers. The relationship would not have been burdened from the beginning by the strains imposed on it by the confusion we both felt.

The pain of being deprived of that first physical contact with my baby, of not having her there for breast-feeding, stayed with me for a long time. Just thinking about it made me feel terrible, as if it had only just happened. It was the pain of having been separated from my child when we needed each other most. For a long time I couldn't talk to anyone about it. It was as if the story of those events was locked up in my own solitude. It was only after I had told Mark about it that I began to free myself from the pressure.

When Carla was a child I couldn't help her; I sensed her anguish but I wasn't able to genuinely communicate with her, support and protect her. I expected her to provide the same things that I had been expected to provide: tacit understanding, faultless functioning, and unblinking acceptance of her fate. But, unlike me, Carla refused to cooperate. She was frequently unable to fulfill even the most basic of expectations, but she never openly rebelled against them. She had too little confidence in herself and sought other people's approval by adopting modes of behavior that I felt were alien to her.

But maybe I was wrong. I wanted to love and understand her, so I wanted to believe that the way she was acting was something she could discard at a later date. At all events, our relationship degenerated into a kind of permanent crisis, largely because she resented my refusal to take the roles she was playing at face value. That was something I couldn't and wouldn't do. I thought I knew who the real Carla was; I felt sure that she had no real need to go through all that playacting, I was certain that it was masking her real, lovable self. I felt the reasons she had for wanting to suppress her real nature were the injuries I had been

a witness to, the injuries inflicted on her whenever she revealed
the person she really was. But just like Max, what she wanted
most was to appear strong, whereas I tormented myself with
feelings of guilt. It took me a long time to stop colluding in that
particular little game because all my life I had been used to taking responsibility for others.

But in Carla's case there was a sense in which I really was to
blame. I felt responsible for the suffering she had been through
in those first few days after she was born. With that uppermost
in my mind, I was bound to see all her reproaches in later life as
justified. I heard in them the voice of the newborn baby unable
to tell me what she was going through except by crying. Today
I know it was a mistake. I had an adult woman in front of me
and all I saw was that poor, helpless, forsaken child she had once
been. It was just like my relationship with Max. For much too
long I thought that in Carla there was a lovable, unspoiled child
trying to get out, a child she refused to let live. And it was with
that child that I kept trying to communicate.

That didn't help Carla at all. It wasn't until I gave up trying
to repair the past that Carla's life eventually took a more settled
course. I finally came to terms with the fact that it was about
time to give up my old pattern of the helpless helper. With my
own daughter it was of course harder than with anyone else. I
had, however, to face up to the fact that it was not in my power
to change the way the consequences of my own fate were
reflected in the lives of my daughters. It was something only
they could contrive to do. My younger daughters found it
much easier than Carla to develop their gifts and make use of
their potential, because the early part of their lives had been
much less stressful. Thanks maybe to the experience of breast-
feeding, they were able to build up a feeling of trust in me from
the outset. And today that has helped them to have far fewer

problems establishing relationships with other people. I hope
that someday Carla will find an empathic partner, someone
with whom she feels secure enough to shake off the artificial
sides of her character and to open up.

That chance encounter with you has stirred up so much that
was dormant in me. But I'm glad. It would have been such a
shame if we'd never heard from each other again. And I'm glad I
could tell you so much about my marriage and the pain in my
relationship with Carla. With my other friends, I've always tried
to defend Max, or else I was ashamed to admit that I had stood
for that intolerable situation so long. Some of my friends even
tried to play the intermediary, to help me to understand Max
better. That was what hurt me most of all. After all, it was my
unending attempts to understand Max that had finally brought
me to much pain.

I had no access to what was really wrong with him. And my
big problem is that my feelings of love wither if I find I can't
understand the other person at all. I was able to tell you all
about the situation I was in because I knew you'd take my part.
I needed you to be biased in my favor. And the fact that you
knew Max also helped. It's only a small and very subjective part
of a long story; but how can you describe the ins and outs of
twenty years of marriage in one single letter?

As far as my relationship with Carla is concerned, I now see
it as a consequence of my speechless childhood and the situation that the marriage to Max put me in. Heredity may also
have played a part, but contemporary geneticists have established
that if a child grows up under optimal conditions it's even possible to change, or at least modify, his or her innate genetic programs. I'm sure that's true. If Carla had had a relaxed, protective,
understanding environment in our family, she would have been
able to develop more trust right from the start. But there was no

way for me of to change her life. Interestingly enough, it was
only after I gave up my struggle and false hope that I have
finally gained more real confidence in Carla's future.

I didn't want to turn all psychological on you; I just wanted
to tell you about the impasses in my life, the blind alleys I've got
stuck in since we parted ways. Fortunately, I managed to get out
of them in the end. And I thank my lucky stars for that.

All the very best from your old—and new—friend,
CLAUDIA

DEAR CLAUDIA,

I was very touched, and very sorry, to hear how much and
how long you suffered in your family. But you have succeeded
in extricating your life from that web of pain. You haven't suc-
cumbed to your distress; you haven't lost courage. Two weeks
ago, in San Diego, you seemed much more outgoing and
relaxed than I remember you being in Berkeley, although you've
had such a tough time of it.

Some people might say, "Don't take life so hard; don't try to
understand all those things there can never be an answer for."
Others might say, "Why do you blame only yourself for all the
things that Carla wasn't given in those first few years? If the
doctors and nurses didn't know how harmful camphor is, how
could you have known? And anyway, the baby had a father,
didn't she? Couldn't he have cuddled the baby and reassured
her? Aren't both parents responsible for their child?"

There may be some truth in all that. But given who you are,
you want to understand your own life as well as you can. And
you certainly have the right. There are plenty of people who
don't seek to make sense of their life. Another thing you say is

that in order to love others you have to be able to understand them. I'm like that myself. That's why I feel close to you, and that's probably why you confided in me. I'm grateful for your trust and I want you to know that I treasure it.

Like yours, my first marriage was also marred by endless misunderstandings. It was less traumatic than your experience, but you certainly couldn't call it fulfilling. I never felt understood, but to be honest I never understood Nicole either. So why did I marry her? For a long time I thought it might have been defiance, to spite you and show you I didn't care that you left me. I wanted a marriage in which I could be more or less sure that I wouldn't be left a second time. But a motive like that is much too weak to sustain a marriage. Soon I felt as if I was in a cage, penned in without the guts to articulate my own wishes, just the way it had been with my mother. I never dared contradict her, either.

In my marriage I had a much starker sense of unease than in my childhood, but I still couldn't put a name to it. Nicole seemed to live in a different world. I felt I was all alone and hopelessly at the mercy of my own feelings. I see that clearly now. With Monica, the relationship is very different: it's genuinely mutual. I always thought that we two had been able to communicate frankly, but when you got involved with Max I started thinking my good memories of you must have been an illusion. I simply couldn't understand you anymore.

Now I see why you tormented yourself with Max all those years, why you put up with an emotional cripple who was unkind to you on top of everything else. For already, as a child, you were expected to cope with things that were too much for you. I'm sure that my childhood was heaven compared with yours. But there were still a couple of things it took me years to work out for myself, notably my relationship with my mother.

But, unlike you, I had brothers and sisters, so I wasn't alone with my family problems.

In my first marriage I always assumed it was my resentment at the things I'd gone through in my childhood that stopped me from understanding Nicole. I often blamed myself, thinking I ought to be able to understand every woman. My mother always expected so much understanding from me. Naturally I was much too young to be able to live up to those expectations, but that didn't stop me from doing the best I could. Since I met Monica, I've realized that those attempts were doomed to failure, the simple reason being that Nicole and I had nothing in common. I still don't understand her, even today, although now that our children are grown and living their own lives we no longer have any reason to get in each other's hair.

My youngest son seems to have interests similar to Nicole's—career, fashion, luxury. Like you, it took me a long time to get over feeling guilty for not having much contact with him after the divorce. After all, if I'd spent more time with him I might have been able to get him interested in things of the mind. But now I realize that he's perfectly entitled to be like his mother, and it's not my fault if he is. The business between you and Carla is much more complicated because it got off on the wrong foot and you blamed yourself for everything. Nothing was going to make you admit that she might also have become like her father. That was probably what hurt you most. I know you and I know Max, so I can imagine why it hit you so hard.

There's nothing we can do to change what we've been through with our children. In the last few years I've been deeply preoccupied with the question of what we can do to avoid unnecessary suffering in very early life or, failing that, to achieve a better understanding so that we can help children to come to terms with it at as early an age as possible.

It's only very recently that scientists have finally come around to admitting the cardinal importance that frequent stroking and massaging has for the development of the infant brain in the first two years of life. It's something that Ashley Montagu was urging almost thirty years ago[2] and a couple of other psychologists also chimed in at the time. But now there are even features on it in *Newsweek*,[3] and that means there's far more likelihood of parents being made to realize how badly their babies need to be in constant physical contact with them. Nicole and I didn't know much about that. As in your own case, it was only later that we became painfully aware of the sins of omission we had unwittingly committed.

It was Monica who first drew my attention to this. She works with midwives and expectant mothers and does what she can to explain the importance of bonding, the direct skin and eye contact between mother and newborn child. It's hard to understand, but despite all the parenting courses and the masses of books for mothers-to-be, there are still thousands of women who have no idea how important the first few minutes after birth are for the child's well-being, both then and later in life. They are entirely ignorant of the fact that a mother who has physical contact with her baby in those first few minutes will find it easier to divine the baby's needs simply by virtue of being "in touch" with him or her. Her body releases hormones that help her to sense what those needs really are. There can be no better foundation for the child's later development.

Monica and I do what we can to spread the word among parents-to-be and the medical and nursing staff at the hospitals. Many adults are simply unaware that a baby is a feeling individual

right from the start. They are skeptical when told how emotionally sensitive babies are, how important it is to take that into
account. The skepticism is understandable; after all, they were
taught as children to be as insensitive as possible in that respect.
Some only acknowledge the fact after they've been in therapy,
and then it's sometimes too late for these insights to do their
children much good. A great deal has been done in the last few
years to make the emotional world of babies and infants better
understood, but it still isn't enough by any means. Some experts
are only just beginning to take the degree of early infant
traumatization in hospitals seriously.

Recently I read a book about circumcision. According to
the author, Ronald F. Goldman,[4] research has shown that more
than 80 percent of the last generation of American males were
routinely circumcised after birth for reasons of "hygiene." Men
rediscovering their early infant emotions in therapy frequently
report that they felt betrayed because their mothers had agreed
to the circumcision. The campaign against this routine procedure was initiated by a number of nurses who refused to have
any part in it.

The author of the book, a physician, quotes a number of
surveys demonstrating how difficult it is to persuade doctors of
the harm done by circumcision. They either deny that it repre-
sents any kind of trauma at all, or they play down the effects it
has. Goldman draws on numerous examples from his everyday
clinical practice to substantiate his theory that many mothers
agree to this medical intervention against their own feelings. For
most of them it was not even associated with any kind of religious convictions, and later they suffered pangs of conscience
about having let it be done to their babies.

One woman reported that after the birth, her son never
cried and was always happy and trusting during breast-feeding.

Then he was taken away from her to be circumcised, and after that nothing was the way it had been before. He cried frequently, refused to breast-feed, and the relationship between them was permanently disturbed. This is doubly tragic after such a promising beginning. What you said about camphor reminded me of this story, and I'm sure there are lots of women who've been through similar experiences.

Today I believe there are two things that are needed: information, of course, but equally—at least in cases of severe abuse—the insight into our own suffering. It is only then that we can accept this vital information and react responsibly to our own situations. Both are mutually reinforcing. Sensitivity to the signals being emitted by newborn babies will presumably come of its own accord once we stop warding off what we know from our own biographies.

There can be no doubt that there would be fewer tragic errors if more were done to disseminate these new insights. But there's a definite risk that this information will go unheeded as long as our feelings are captive to total amnesia. Intellectual knowledge alone is not enough; that kind of knowledge does not penetrate to the level of our actual behavior, our actions. But strong emotional experiences can do precisely that. And these emotions will inevitably be released when people start telling a sympathetic person they trust about their own childhood. Today there are even video features that prove the point.

There's a documentary by a Japanese television team I saw. Hardened criminals, murderers most of them, who have never allowed themselves to have any feelings, are given group therapy during which they talk about their childhood. It's amazing to see how much emotion is reflected in their faces as they do so. Many are able to cry for the first time in their lives, to grieve over their own personal fate and what they have done to their

victims. They begin to realize that the murders they have committed were attempts to escape from what they are now feeling.

When you see those faces change, you suddenly realize that
no amount of reading or press coverage could ever have had the
same effect as the eruption of long-lost feelings in the presence
of someone who is genuinely willing to listen. Only now are
they able to understand why they did something they never
wanted to do; only now are they receptive to information that
can help them to avoid committing similar acts in the future.
The implacable repression of their feelings kept them captive
not only to their own ignorance but also to the danger they
represented for society and for themselves.

It is very painful to be confronted with the sufferings of our
childhood. So I can well understand why many people choose a
different path and just don't want to know. But I'm glad that
not everybody opts for that course, and I'm glad that we've met
again after all these years. In Berkeley there were lots of barriers
between us, but it looks as if deep down we've always been similar. It's just that when we were younger we were not free
enough to live our lives the way we really were.

All my love,
DANIEL

YOLANTA AND LINDA

Really Welcome

Dear Mary,

I'm writing to you on the flight from Los Angeles to Chicago. We're just flying over the Grand Canyon, and I have a few hours to myself before the routine of life back home gets a hold on me again.

You know I went to Los Angeles to see Doris. She used to be a close friend of mine, but then she went to train as a midwife and I haven't seen her for ages.

After working as a hospital midwife for a number of years, Doris decided that what she really wanted to do was to work with women having their children at home and prepare them psychologically. So she set herself up in a practice of her own and did just that. While I was there, she told me about one

mother who had had two Caesareans and then got pregnant for
the third time. Thanks to Doris, she was able to work in the
garden right up to the time when the labor pains set in. She was
taken to Doris's place, and two hours after she got there the
child was born. Her neighbor could hardly believe her eyes
when she saw her arriving back home only a few hours later
with her baby in her arms.

Doris offered to take me along to one of her home births.
And that's the main reason why I'm writing you this letter.

The child's name is Yolanta, and the whole family had been
looking forward to her birth for months. The parents were
happy to be having a baby girl at last and had prepared their
two boys, aged two and four, for the event.

The birth itself was uncomplicated. The newborn baby
didn't cry; she just lay on her mother's stomach and looked up
curiously at her face. The mother was radiant, caressing her tiny
daughter, and she couldn't take her eyes off her. The baby wasn't
bathed or given any injections; she was just left lying quietly
where she was and slowly learning to regulate her own breath-
ing. She didn't even cry when the umbilical cord was cut; she
just took a deep breath. Not so long ago it was normal for
babies to be held up by the feet so that they could breathe better. No one realized what a shock this was for them. When they
cried, this was taken to be a sign that the lungs had started functioning properly. Why are we humans always trying to improve
on nature, although things work perfectly well if they're allowed
to take a natural course?

Yolanta was an avid breast-feeder right from the start.
Between meals she slept and cried only when she was hungry.
As soon as her mother gave her the breast, she immediately
calmed down again. After five days, Doris took the first blood
sample. This involved pricking Yolanta in the sole of her foot,

and Doris decided to do it immediately after the baby had finished feeding. With babies, Doris said, a pain of this kind should never be inflicted on an empty stomach. The infant should be happy, sated, and lying in its mother's arms. Doris conscientiously observed all these points. But even then, the sudden pain shook the little body through and through, almost like an electric shock, although the whole procedure lasted no longer than a minute. It looked as if all was well finally. Yolanta was quiet for a moment, but then she suddenly started crying again. This time my impression was that her cries had a different quality; it wasn't just a physical reaction to a physical pain. It was like an expression of profound despair somehow connected with the prick of the needle and the emotional confusion it had plunged her into. Her mother tried everything she knew to console her—gave her the breast, cradled her, stroked her. But all these demonstrations of love were to no avail.

Yolanta was not prepared for an assault of this kind; she had no program to deal with it, no ready-made natural response. It was as if her body had to vent itself of all the disappointment at this sudden painful attack on it, as if this tiny person were saying, "What have I done wrong? I've been feeding at mother's breast like a good girl. For five days everything was fine. What happened? Why do I get pierced all of a sudden? I don't understand how this world works, what it has in store for me; everything suddenly seems mysterious and threatening. All I can do is make as much noise as I can. There were no pains like this in my mother's womb. Will they come back again the next time I'm feeding?"

The physical pain had long since ebbed away, but Yolanta was still protesting with all her might against this attack. Does a trauma like this leave traces? Probably not, as long as Yolanta is put back in the arms of a mother who has the patience to give her all the reassurance she needs. Her mother looked down on her tenderly and with a certain pride that her daughter could assert herself in this way. Perhaps when she grows up, her daughter will be able to look after herself better than her mother ever could.

Ten minutes later, Yolanta stopped crying. Doris massaged her little body. Yolanta's first response was wary, then she started to enjoy the pressure of Doris's hands. She also seemed to relish the bath she was given a little later, though the look she gave Doris still betrayed a degree of caution and suspicion. Before the blood sample, there had been none of this wariness in her eyes. The puncturing of the skin was obviously a shock for the baby, but thanks to the mother's sensitivity, Doris's experienced care, and the sympathy of her brothers, who came in and cuddled their little sister, Yolanta seemed to get over the experience fairly quickly.

You've no idea how often I thought back to your birth while I was watching all this. I would have loved to have my children in such an atmosphere. Seeing Yolanta come into the world reinforced all the dismay I still feel at having been so ill-prepared. But at the same time it reconciled me with what I had been through. It's a consolation to know that you and other young mothers will have the benefit of something that I was denied. Today, we know so much more, and you have your own ideas about what you want, too.

When I think how inexperienced I was when I was expecting my first child, I simply cannot believe that I didn't try to find out more about what I was in for. When I felt what I thought were the first labor pains, Daddy dropped everything and drove me twenty miles to the hospital. He was afraid we'd get there too late. They prepared me for the birth as if I was to undergo major surgery, and then I was put on a clean white bed. Because it all reminded me of the last operation I'd been through, I became apprehensive, then frightened, and finally really panicky. The whole procedure probably also reminded me of the trauma of my own birth.

I know now, because Doris told me, that it's not unusual for pregnant women to get rogue labor pains a few days before the birth, but they go away again once the midwife has made sure that the birth won't be for a few days yet. But in the hospital there was no one there to reassure me, and I was exposed to an immense amount of stress that no one took the time to talk to me about. I felt completely incapable of performing the task I was there to perform and spent my days in dread of not being able to live up to the expectations of the doctors and the nursing staff. As a result, my whole body went rigid and the labor pains subsided altogether.

Actually it was a good thing that you decided to wait. You obviously didn't want to come into the world as long as your mother was so afraid. I was discharged from the hospital, went on long walks with your father, and finally relaxed. And then on the third day, the labor pains started in earnest, the birth canal started opening, and only a few hours later you were born quite normally, with no trouble at all.

How long will it take for something so obviously right to assert itself and for women to refuse to be persuaded of the opposite?

They're coming 'round with the meals now. I'm glad I've had the chance to write to you like this. I'll call as soon as I'm back in Chicago.

Your loving
MOM

DEAR MOM,

It's been a long time since you last wrote. Your trip to Los
Angeles seems to have done you a world of good. You often
mentioned the circumstances of my birth before, but somehow
I always closed my ears. Probably I felt bad about your guilt
feelings. You were so unhappy about the labor pains coming and
going, and then you told me that the birth took three days and
must have been a traumatic experience for me. That scared me.
I started feeling I was responsible for the contractions stopping
and for not releasing you from your fears quickly enough. That
put an awful strain on me. Also, I felt I had to console you and
forgive you so that you could finally free yourself of your guilty
conscience. It was a vicious circle, because your guilt probably
originated from your own childhood. Nothing I could do or
say would ever make any difference.

I'm really glad that you've got over all that agonizing about
my birth. For years I've been trying to teach myself not to see
your problems as my own, and I'm getting better at it. But now
that I'm going to be a mother in two months' time myself, it's a
real weight off my mind and I'm really grateful to Doris and
Yolanta for these new experiences you've been having. It wasn't
your fault that there was no one to help you when you were in
the hospital.

Now, twenty-five years later, and thanks to Doris, you've
finally found out that there's nothing unusual about labor pains
stopping and starting. But it wasn't my fault either. I obviously
just decided to bide my time until you had calmed down. Now
that I've realized that, I see the whole business of my birth in a
completely new light. Instead of seeing myself as passive and
timid, I now have this image of myself as someone who knew
how to avoid danger and get her own way even before she was

born. If I'd been born while you were panicking, who knows what would have become of me! Luckily they sent you back home from the hospital and gave you time to relax. It would have been much worse if they'd given you something to induce the birth artificially.

No one ever used to bother thinking about the psychological effects of that kind of interference. If a child was born autistic, they looked for some genetic reason and never asked themselves whether something awful might not have happened to it in the uterus. Lots of hospitals refuse to deliver babies at weekends. That means that now they can force babies to come into the world on workdays only. And if all else fails, there's always a Caesarean section. That seems to have come back into fashion again.

But there are doctors willing to supervise births at home. And in the process they learn something that no one ever talked to them about during their medical training: respect for the feelings of women having a baby. I've found myself a doctor like that. She's not only a physician; she's also a midwife and the mother of several children herself. She's watched more than a thousand home births. Ralph will be there of course, and we don't have to rush off to the hospital in a frenzy. We'll just wait quietly at home for our baby to arrive, and there'll be an expert midwife on hand in case she's needed. And that's all.

Right now, before the baby is even born, we're aware that we won't always manage to be so adult toward our child, as uninhibited and as free from anxieties as we'd like to be. No one can guarantee that in certain situations the old hang-ups won't suddenly reassert themselves, the ones we haven't integrated into our awareness. But when that happens, it helps if your partner doesn't get all uptight and demand things that you just can't give at that moment.

This is not just a theory I've read somewhere; it's part of our married life. You know that Ralph's father was cruel to him, and on many occasions I've seen him overwhelmed by the fear of being rejected and humiliated for the most trivial reasons. I know now that when that happens, the last thing I must do is give in to the temptation to react impatiently or helplessly. I wait until Ralph has found his way back to reality and stops seeing me as his violent father or the mother who abandoned him. I know that he won't stay that way for long. And I can hold out because Ralph tells me frankly what's going on inside him and doesn't hide behind a mask to preserve some illusion of power and mastery.

I hope that with this kind of trust to build on we won't ever expect our child to free us from our own anxieties. She would never be able to, and anyway it's not her job. When I was a child, I spent ages trying to free you of your fears and the result was that I took them on myself. That was no help to me or you. I'm glad to have found someone like Ralph who doesn't take advantage of my tendency to take on other people's suffering, to feel by proxy, vicariously, what someone else doesn't want to feel. He has decided to live with his feelings and to come to terms with them, however difficult that may sometimes be. He can tell me about them, describe them to me, but he has no urge to unload them on me and make me responsible for them. You can imagine what a new experience that is for me and how liberating it is.

So you see, I was preparing for the birth of our child before you went to Los Angeles. Your letter has come as an extra gift. You probably went to see Doris to get the latest information on childbirth for me. It's a pity you didn't go to Los Angeles much earlier, for your own sake. But that kind of thing obviously takes time. Better late than never. I'm looking forward to seeing you.

I'm no longer afraid of your feelings, which means I'm no longer afraid for my baby either. It takes the pressure off our relationship and it makes me very happy.

All my love,
MARY

DEAR DORIS,

I found the time we spent together in Los Angeles so fulfill-ing that I wrote a long letter about Yolanta to my daughter Mary as soon as I was on the plane. I've been back in Chicago for several weeks now, and I've been lucky enough to be present at a home birth right here. Naturally I want to see what you think of my highly unqualified conclusions!

The young mother was Anna, the daughter of a good friend of mine who died a tragic death some time ago. I had told her about meeting you in Los Angeles, and she asked me to be present at the birth. The circumstances could hardly have been better. Anna's husband, Robert, was very sensitive, very caring, held her close whenever he could. I really had the feeling they were going through the whole thing together. They'd both been greatly looking forward to having the baby and had no reserva-tions whatsoever. The position of the baby was quite normal.

So with everything going for an easy birth, the midwife was very surprised that the initial phase took almost ten hours. Even then the opening hadn't dilated enough. I went away into the next room because I suddenly thought my being there might remind Anna of her mother's death and those sad memories might be preventing her from entering joyfully and whole-heartedly into the birth process. When the midwife joined me, I asked her what she thought. She was a very open-minded and

understanding woman, but she said it wasn't a good idea to start
asking someone in labor questions of that kind; there was obviously something getting in the way of things, but it couldn't be
anything conscious or we wouldn't be having this trouble. Her
suggestion was to give Anna something homeopathic to help
her relax.

When Robert came in for a moment, I asked him what he
thought. As a layperson, he had no preconceived notions and he
thought it would be a good idea to ask Anna outright whether
she would prefer me not to be there. But when he did, she said
it was absolutely not the case and burst out crying. Obviously it
wasn't her mother's death that was causing her to seize up like
that. It turned out to be something that she had told Robert
about years ago but which had haunted her throughout her
pregnancy. And now she was fighting against herself to keep the
awful memories at bay, and the effort was taking up almost all
the energy she needed for her baby and the birth.

When she was fifteen, she and a school friend of hers had
been gang-raped. She told her parents all about it, and their
support and concern had given her comfort and strength. But
now, as it all came flooding back, she felt alone because she had
told herself it wasn't the time and place to talk about such
things. Maybe Robert had also been obeying the unwritten law
that one should never talk to a woman in labor. But now all it
needed was for him to ask how she was feeling and she stopped
trying to blot it out. She let him take her in his arms and cried
and cried.

It was those tears that helped her to relax. She realized that
she had been afraid to open herself and she knew now why she
had been afraid. Her body was anticipating another catastrophe;
it feared that if it opened, something terrible would happen.

The birth process had reactivated the unconscious fear of a repetition of the trauma. The hours of keening she had been through had nothing to do with the labor pains; they were a sign that without knowing it, she was suffering from the pain left by the humiliation and helplessness she had felt all those years ago. Once she knew that she was no longer alone with that pain, it took only a few minutes for the contractions to set in. Half an hour later her baby was born. No medication, no incision, in a squatting position, almost without pain.

If she had been in the hospital, they might not have waited that long. Out of concern for the child, they might have decided to perform a Caesarean section, something which Anna, who wanted a natural birth above all else, might have experienced as an act of violence. Tell me, why do we go to such lengths to avoid talking to each other and asking questions? Are we afraid of the answers we might get? This well-meaning reticence is not always a good thing. It may mean that a woman in labor, surrounded by her loved ones, can get sucked down into a feeling of immense solitude just as she is being assailed by traumatic memories from within her own body.

I can well imagine that the interest shown by someone you love or anyone there who's sensitive can release you from your isolation and help you to come to terms with whatever is troubling you. What do you think?

I also learned a great deal from baby Linda's behavior immediately after birth. First she looked around as if to make sure there were no dangers in the offing, and, like Yolanta, she didn't cry when the umbilical cord was cut. At the breast she recognized her mother immediately, reached for the nipple, and even started sucking. But, over and over again, she stopped feeding

and cried bitterly. I had the feeling that those sobs racking her
little body were telling her story about those long hours she had
spent in the birth canal, without anyone to turn to, all alone in
the dark. Her mother had us all around her bed, comforting her
in her pain. As an adult, she knew that it would all come to an
end sometime, probably quite soon. She was ideally prepared for
what was coming. All the same, the waiting had been an ordeal.

How much more of an ordeal that waiting must be for the
child, I thought. A baby has no idea what is happening: the time
has come for her to make her entrance, and yet she still has to
wait for hours, sensing the mother's fear, unable to do anything
to change position as long as the mother is all tensed up. The
baby has no way of knowing that everything will probably be
all right, no idea what's in store. I could imagine that when the
release finally comes, crying is a baby's way of telling what she's
been through. There's no other way. Crying is the only language
she knows.

In the right kind of supportive surroundings, the baby can
obviously get over the birth trauma very quickly. Linda cried for
some time, almost an hour, but in the following days she cried
only very rarely, when she was hungry, and stopped immediately
when she was given the breast.

I met Anna and Robert a number of times after that. They
are very happy parents, and they say that Linda keeps them
posted about her needs, telling them in no uncertain terms
what she wants, and no messing around. They find it astonishing. I don't. Linda senses unerringly that both her parents want
to understand her. She knows she can trust them.

Now I'm greatly looking forward to the birth of my first
grandchild. Like Linda, this will be another baby with the
immense good fortune of having well-informed, loving parents.

Doris, I can't thank you enough for the new world you

opened up for me. I'm so much clearer in my mind now than I was before.

All my love,
LISA

DEAR LISA,

Thanks for your letter. It looks like you're getting to be quite an expert in my line of work! And a good thing, too. Information is everything! Sins of omission in the first two years are sometimes irremediable. The "work of mourning" you observed baby Linda going through is a well-known phenomenon. Some children need days before they get through it, even if things are going well. But if they are exposed to some new trauma, treated badly, separated from the mother, weaned for no good reason, then of course their crying will have a number of different meanings, not always easy to interpret.

From what you tell me about the midwife's reaction to your suggestion, I would guess she was simply assuming that a woman in labor is not usually thinking about the past so much as what is going on right now. Normally she will be concerned for the child and nothing else and wants to do everything possible to bring it into the world with as little stress as possible. But many women are worried that they will not be equal to the demands of the situation, and that initial apprehension can turn into panic and fear as the labor pains get more extreme. The fear of not being up to it is compounded by the fear of the pain, which reawakens memories in the body of earlier pains it has suffered.

In this case, the mother-to-be's conscious mind is still cut off from her past. But at the unconscious level, memories of earlier traumatic experiences are being activated. The site where the old dramas are reenacted is the body. Like you, I believe that in that situation it can be helpful to have someone there asking sympathetic questions that can bridge the gap between the birth situation and earlier experiences.

As soon as I started my job, I was struck by the fact that women who had been sexually abused in their earlier lives frequently had a harder time relaxing during the birth process. Some were indeed quite simply afraid to "open themselves," but there were lots of others who willed their bodies into such a state of insensitivity that the birth was over very quickly. It was as if they were trying to rid themselves of the burden as fast as they could. These mothers at first displayed a high degree of indifference toward their babies. Their self-imposed physical and mental insensitivity helped them ward off the painful memories. But it was only when they were able to talk about what had happened to them in their childhood that they could really open their hearts to their new baby.

This is why I do all I can to get at those early traumatizations by talking to the mothers before the birth. The women are usually grateful for the chance to talk about it, and I believe these exchanges do a great deal to make the actual labor period easier to get through. Very definitely part of the job, I'd say.

All my best wishes for you and Mary. Please write to me and tell me how she's feeling.

All my love,
DORIS

DEAR DORIS,

Mary's baby has arrived! It's a girl; her name is Nina, and of course I'm completely enchanted by her. Not just because she's my first grandchild. Everything about her tells me that a human being just starting out in life is equipped with healthy instincts that even in a world like ours can function wonderfully well as long as they're allowed to. And that certainty fills me with new optimism.

Nina is four weeks old now. At first she was mostly quiet and happy, slept soundly and drank her fill at her mother's breast. Now she's starting to look around and smile a lot. If there's something troubling her, if it's too cold or too hot or she has a stomachache, she cries. Mary always seems to know why she's crying and can comfort her very quickly. But if Mary isn't immediately on hand, the crying sometimes turns into a desperate wailing that seems to contain all the earlier pain she's been through, including, presumably, the trauma of birth itself. But as soon as she's given the breast, all is well again.

What really bowls me over is her particular brand of logic. It all seems to be dictated by nature and hence to be completely self-evident. It's marvelous to see that parents can give so much to their child, and hence to society, simply by deciding to be so totally and unconditionally there for her in those first days and weeks, the way Mary and Robert are.

All my love,
LISA

ANIKA

Worth a Try

ANIKA'S MOTHER has been divorced for many years. Today she lives in an old people's home. Her daughter, now well into her forties, studied Romance languages and teaches at a secondary school in Budapest. She has come to see her mother where she now lives. She is glad to be visiting her in neutral surroundings free of any childhood memories. In fact, she finds the impersonal way the room is furnished oddly appropriate to the character of her mother. Even when she lived at home, there was hardly anything personal about the place. Her mother always left the interior decoration to others—her daughters or the people who worked for her. All her life she behaved in many ways like a child that needed to be looked after. The cold, anonymous atmosphere of this institution obviously does not upset her in any way.

During Anika's visits it is usual for the conversation to revolve around her mother's concerns. Anika has never talked about her own life, and her mother has never inquired about it. Whenever her daughter volunteers information about herself, her mother has immediately interrupted her with lamentations about her own worries. But today Anika has resolved to stick to her guns.

Once the usual greetings have been exchanged, she sails in without any further ado. "Shall I tell you something, Mother," she says. "I've suddenly realized something. My main aim in life has always been to make sure that you're happy. And doing that meant organizing your life for you, to make sure that you were all right. But I never succeeded. I always felt guilty, obscurely obliged to be doing something for you, but I never knew what would have made you happy. The result was permanent stress, unremitting exhaustion, disappointment with myself, because I never achieved the goal I had set myself."

"Did I ever make you responsible for the position I was in? It wasn't your fault that I hated the Communist regime and that your father divorced me. We were living under difficult conditions."

"Yes, you were always complaining about them. That was what made me want to free you from them, to change those conditions, help you emigrate somewhere else where you'd be happier, better off. But whatever I tried, I always failed because I couldn't get you to make a decision. You hated the government, dreamed of other countries; but in the last resort you didn't want to be away from your grown-up children. So you never seriously contemplated leaving Budapest. I was the only one who took your emigration plans seriously, and that was why I entered into all that correspondence with people in the West. I went on racking my brains for a solution that simply couldn't exist."

"Why not?"

"No daughter in the world could ever have satisfied your longing for shelter and togetherness, for a nice, cozy home. Instead of creating such a place yourself, you foisted off your parental functions onto your children, although you were supposed to be the adult. We did what we could to fulfill them. But you were never satisfied because deep down you were still suffering from the things you had been through as a child and later denied ever having existed."

"I don't know what you're talking about. My parents loved me; so did my brothers and sisters. I had a wonderful youth."

"That can't be true. If that were true, you'd have been able to pass that love on to me, as well. All the illusions, all the lies that we live by are fine as long as they do us good. But sometimes the price they demand is high, and often enough it's the children who have to pay it. But you certainly haven't got off scot free yourself. The price you've had to pay is the panic and fear that has been hounding you for years. When you were young, you managed to ward it off."

"What fear? What are you talking about? I never had any fears when I was young."

"You compensated for your fears by exercising power over me."

"Those are strong words you're using. I had to bring you up, didn't I? And that's not something you can postpone till later. Start as you mean to go on; otherwise a child will soon turn into a tyrant. You had definite tendencies in that direction; you always wanted to have your own way. But I persevered, and in the end I taught you how to behave. I taught you not to be selfish, to think of others first and yourself last and so forth. In time you learned all that and grew up into a reasonably presentable young girl. You ought to be grateful. I'm sure it's helped you to get on well in life."

"Mother," Anika says, quietly but firmly, "you've often hurt me by saying things like that about upbringing and so on. I couldn't see any way of bridging the gap between us. But today I know only too well that any woman tormenting her children with these absurd ideas on proper upbringing must have had an awful childhood herself. Mind you, I'm quite aware that you thought you were doing your duty, that you were doing your best to be a good mother."

"How am I supposed to have tormented you then?"

"If you really want to know, I can read you a letter you wrote me after I'd started my psychoanalysis and asked you what I was like as a child. I had no memories at all of that period myself. Do you want to hear it? I have it here with me."

"Yes, go ahead."

"In this letter you say: 'When you were eight years old, we both took German lessons with a neighbor, a teacher at the local high school. One day he gave us an essay to write as homework. He was very approving about what you had written, but he wasn't very complimentary about my efforts. Then you made a remark that really made me cross. Back home I let off steam and threatened to give you a licking you wouldn't forget for the rest of your born days. You ran around the table, with me after you. But you were quicker and I couldn't get hold of you. So I put my coat on and left the house. When I came back in the evening, you just sat there looking at me. After a while it got on my nerves. You asked me what I was going to do next, and I said you'd better go to bed since I hadn't decided how I was going to punish you. One thing was for sure, though, I was going to talk to your principal about you and see what she advised. At last you went to bed. When I woke up the next morning and looked in on you, you were sitting up in bed and stared at me all wide-eyed and started asking your interminable questions again. You said you hadn't had a wink of sleep because you didn't know what was going to happen. As always, your constant questions irritated me, and I told you to get yourself off to school. You said you were afraid you might meet your principal, and I said it served you right if you were scared—it was no less than you deserved. After that I didn't say a word to you for ten days. The punishment worked like a charm. You turned over a new leaf, stopped running off everywhere with your school friends, and stayed home with me. I needed your company because your father already had a mistress and I was lonely. After that incident I never had any trouble with you again.' "

"I can't remember writing that letter, but I remember the episode very well. It was you who tormented me, not the other way around, asking all those questions I couldn't answer. I really didn't know what the best kind of punishment would be because I was very hurt by what you said."

"Well, what did I say?"

"I can't remember."

"Maybe I wasn't the one who hurt you. Maybe you were so devastated by what the teacher said that you took it out on me instead?"

"I don't know. All I know is that I would have dearly loved to go to secondary school, but my father wouldn't let me. That teacher made me feel ashamed and exposed."

"With your methods of upbringing, you did everything you could to turn me into what you called a 'noble character.' But unconsciously you were prey to the indomitable urge to let out all your pent-up feelings on me. You were never aware of what was really behind the anger you felt about me. That letter doesn't say a word about what I'm supposed to have said to hurt you so much. It's like Kafka's *Trial.* Nobody tells me what I've done wrong. Maybe I never said anything at all—what reason would I

have had? The teacher had said it all. You probably couldn't per-
mit yourself to be angry with him, and even if you had, you
could never have said so. Instead you could take out your anger
on me with impunity. So subjectively you experienced me as an
aggressor, maybe like your father or your brother when you
were a child. And because you believed in tough upbringing
methods and your power over me was more or less limitless, you
decided corporal punishment was the solution.

"That 'solution' worked till I was eight or so. After that I
must have managed to escape your blows. But my psychological distress was there still. You kept me in the dark, threatened
to embarrass me at school, the only place where I had any
refuge. And all for offenses I didn't know I'd committed. That
way you could keep me in a constant state of guilt. I was afraid
of doing things—unintentionally, unwittingly—that might
hurt you. I tried to find out the things I should avoid doing.
But as you yourself write, my questions got on your nerves,
the way I looked at you was unnerving, my desire to find out
the true reason for your anger was nothing but indecent cu-
riosity. I saw myself as 'bad' when I asked you about the things
I'd done wrong, because you never gave me a satisfactory answer. I felt an overwhelming need for clarity, but I experienced that need as something threatening because you
couldn't take it. It was bound to end in complications, maybe
even disaster.

"For a long time I felt the only way not to put too much of
a burden on our relationship was to say nothing, to conceal what
I felt. That was the best way of getting along with you. But my
encounters with other people showed me that not everybody
reacted to my questions in that strange way. I met people who
were actively grateful for being asked things. Gradually I grew
out of my timidity. It was a long, painful process. And it's a

process that people who get listened to when they're young don't have to go through."

"When I was a girl, I had to keep my mouth shut and do as I was told."

"I'm sure you did. 'Speech is silver, silence is golden'—that was your motto as a mother, wasn't it? For me, having to be silent was doubly tragic because it neutralized all my energy, my trust, my capacity for love. In those self-help books they keep on telling you to love yourself. But how can you love yourself if from the word 'go,' you have it brought home to you that your mother finds your longing for contact, truth, understanding to be annoying, personally offensive, or even actively dangerous?

"That's not something you can just shake off; gradually, you arrive at the unconscious conviction that you have to suppress these cravings for any kind of connection if you want to get along with people. So then you start smothering your most natural impulses, and when people advise you to love yourself, you end up asking whom you're supposed to love. You don't even know who you are; you only know one tiny part of your own nature.

"People learn to recognize themselves in the eyes of their mother. The French word *merveille,* miracle, always reminds me of a combination of *mère* (mother) and *veille* (awake), and if you look at it that way, it seems like a reflection of that insight. But I can't remember ever getting one single glance from you that was really meant for me, as opposed to being steeped in your notions about what I ought to be like. When I look back, I have this vision of your eyes resting on a point somewhere behind me, as if you were looking through me all the time."

"I can't remember my mother ever looking at me at all. When she wasn't at work, she devoted herself entirely to my father. It was the servants who looked after us children, and they kept on changing. I can't remember any one of them."

"Maybe that's the reason why you never really saw me at all. In talking about the way you function, I'm not trying to hurt you; I'm trying to understand our life together. That letter of yours carries a covert explanation, one it took me a long time to detect. Lots of nasty things had to happen before I finally summoned up the courage to face up to that letter and all its implications. The letter shows exactly how you were programming me for my role in life. What it says in effect is 'You, Anika, are bad and selfish when you go off and have fun with your friends and leave me alone with my depression. You have hurt me and you deserve severe punishment. The only way you can escape that punishment is by exclusively and uninterruptedly devoting yourself to my welfare and relieving me of my worries, including the responsibility for your younger brother and sister.' "

The more Anika gets into her stride, the stronger she feels. Suddenly she has the courage to face things that she has never spoken about to her mother—or anyone else.

"As the end of the letter shows, I did what you wanted. The extent to which your motherly maxims seeped into me was something I never even so much as suspected up until quite recently. I internalized your messages so completely that I kept on letting myself be manipulated in the same way. All anyone had to do was arouse my compassion or accuse me of hurting them, and that was it, the game was over, checkmate. Flattery cut no ice with me; hypocrisy I was inordinately allergic to—but compassion and guilt feelings always caught me off guard. If others were suffering, I was the first to seek the reasons for it in myself. My efforts to enhance other people's well-being were tireless. Only when I had the feeling that the person in question was strong enough and sincere enough for a confrontation did I manage to defend myself.

"If I'd been able to start thinking clearly and uninhibitedly at an early stage, my life would have taken a different course. Instead, I kept on reacting the way I had when I was eight. I wanted to see you happy and satisfied. It was a goal I pursued for thirty years, sometimes at great cost to myself and invariably to the detriment of my true feelings and my health. And all because I wanted to free you of whatever tormented you and finally live in peace myself."

"Aren't you exaggerating the role I played in your life? I never had the feeling I was very important to you."

"Of course there were other influences. But we're talking here about our relationship. And the role of the mother is important in everyone's life. We always had someone to look after us, true, but you still kept me under constant personal surveillance. I did everything you wanted, assuming that if I did, you would finally come to love me. My whole life revolved around you. I may never have told you that, you may never have realized it, but that's the way it was."

"Are you saying I never loved you? Maybe I did love you less than your brother. My father had been looking forward to a grandson. When you were born, I admit I was disappointed."

"I must have sensed that, I suppose, but I never felt hated, just constantly unsure of myself. I never knew what your feelings for me were. I felt manipulated, and all the time I believed I ought to be different from the way I was because then you'd finally start liking me. I don't even imagine that you were so unyielding to me because you were severe by nature. Maybe you were unconsciously imitating your father. By breaking my spirit you could build up your own again. Lots of the things about your father that made you suffer—his obsession with power, his lack of understanding—were things you took out on me. You've never admitted it, but your behavior toward me has lots of similarities to the way Grandfather behaved toward you. I might have been able to escape your manipulations if I hadn't let you saddle me with the responsibility for looking after you."

"Shall I tell you something? I was top of the class in elementary school, but they still wouldn't let me attend secondary school. And that hurt. I was always jealous of you because you were given something I'd been denied. That jealousy may have been part of why I was so angry with you after what happened with the German teacher. But I still gave you every encouragement with regard to your education."

"That's true, and I'm grateful to you for it. I always felt supported by you, throughout my schooling; in that respect you were a good mother. Maybe because the pain you felt at being so poorly educated yourself was the only one you were willing to countenance, the only one you were aware of. That made you want to save me from a similar fate. But you repressed all the other deprivations and humiliations you were exposed to as a child so completely that you took them out on me unconsciously. It's all in that letter."

"What exactly are you talking about?"

"You were one of a family of twelve children, all born in quick succession. I imagine you were neglected."

"Maybe you're right. I suffered as a child without ever admitting it to myself. I thought that everything that had happened to me was because I was bad and immoral. I was convinced I was to blame for it all."

"Yes, and to get rid of those guilt feelings once and for all, you visited them on me. From my earliest years I felt I was to blame for your fears, although I didn't know the reason for them. What I wanted most in the world was to free you of them.

By denying your own childhood distress, you heaped a tremendous burden onto my shoulders. And you practically made me
into the mother of my brother and sister, foisting the responsibility for them onto me when I was still a little girl."

"Until today I was proud of having brought you up so well. All
your successes I regarded as if they were my own. Now you come
along and take that away from me; you call it all an illusion."

"And it never occurred to you that your children were paying the price?"

"No. And I'm still not entirely convinced that it's true. That's
your view. There are others. But you seem to be so determined
to stick to your opinions that I'm not going to argue with you. I
just don't believe you can change the world. You're tilting at
windmills."

"I don't believe you can change the world either; I don't
even believe you can change one single person. You can only
change yourself and then only if you really want to. But if parents want to give their children a better chance than they had
themselves, there are much better ways today of discovering how
to go about it. Forty years ago it was considered quite normal to
hit your children. It's still done today, but not everywhere and
not with such a clear conscience. That in itself is a step in the
right direction.

"I used to think that as a professional educator, as the author
of a child care manual, you were bound to be interested in such
developments. But you're a product of your time, and I can
imagine you would be distressed if you really faced up to the issues involved in parent–child relationships. You might end up realizing that when I was still a baby I was the first person you ever
tried asserting yourself with. With your brothers and your father
you wouldn't have had a ghost of a chance. That insight would

be a painful one. And today I can understand that you don't want that kind of pain; you think you just couldn't handle it.

"But the fact that we've been able to talk like this, the fact that you've listened to me shows that you could have been a good mother if before I was born you had been better informed about what a child really needs, instead of being misguided by all those old notions about good upbringing. You've been good to me in lots of ways, whatever I may have said, otherwise I wouldn't be here now. I'm glad we could talk, even if we don't see eye to eye on many things."

Anika is saddened when she takes leave of her mother. She realizes that the childish hope of being able to explain something to her mother, to "teach" her something about herself, is still there deep down within her. At times her mother appeared interested, ready to take an active part in the exchange. And that misled Anika into falling back on the old pattern and showing her mother the compassion she felt for her unfulfilled life. But in retrospect the grown-up Anika realizes that all her efforts have been to no avail. Nothing has changed. At some points her mother did appear to sit up and take note, but the fate of her daughter still leaves her largely indifferent. The prevailing emotion was one of fear, fear of genuinely understanding the connections Anika was trying to show existed between their two lives. She remains caught up in the notions she has lived by and seems happy to stay that way in her old age. Anika realizes that there is no point in trying to chip away at those notions any longer and in repeating such conversations. But the grief she now feels tells her that her work is not yet over. Little Anika's justfied rage at her "perfect" mother will certainly reassert itself, and after this encounter the adult Anika will have an even better understanding of the child she once was.

HELGA

Trading on Tears

HELGA, a trained social worker in her late thirties, lives and works in Los Angeles. Eight years ago, she signed up for a therapy program. After an interview with the director of the clinic, she was admitted immediately, although the information material had warned that applicants might have to wait several years. On the one hand, her quick admission and the director's suggestive remarks about her good looks flattered her. But she also found the whole thing vaguely suspicious. She decided to ignore her misgivings. After separating from her partner, she had been in a state of considerable distress, feeling as if she had been left all alone in the world with her one-year-old daughter. So she was pleased that the man who ran the center had found her attractive. Above all, she was relieved that she could start therapy right away, because she had developed a dependency on sleeping pills and found this very alarming.

In the first stages of therapy she cried a lot. This phase lasted for weeks. The therapist said very little, but it was good for someone to be there listening to everything she told him. She was told that she could call at any time if she felt her fears and anxieties were overwhelming her, and she made use of this opportunity on a number of occasions. Once when she called, her therapist was not at home and his wife answered the phone. Quite without warning, she volunteered an astonishingly frank account of what she was going through with her husband, one of her accusations being that he exploited the dependency of young female patients to indulge in sex games with them, systematically neglecting and humiliating her in the process.

Helga terminated the conversation quickly because she didn't want to hear any slanderous remarks about her "savior." In retrospect, she admits that at the time she wasn't even shocked by these revelations. Her trust in the therapy was implicit, and she interpreted the incident as an expression of the wife's jealousy and her envy of younger women. When she told the therapist about the call, he appeared neither indignant nor surprised but explained calmly that his wife was an alcoholic, that she made up stories about him and didn't know what she was saying when she'd been drinking. He described her as inordinately possessive and jealous, but he felt sorry for her and didn't want to leave her after thirty years of marriage, now that she was so mixed up. All he hoped was that she could kick the habit because she was harming not only him but herself as well.

Helga forgot all about the phone call, not even recalling it when she first entered into sexual relations with her therapist. She went on believing everything he told her and felt loved and gratified that his choice had fallen on her. This enhanced her feelings of self-esteem so much that she spent several weeks in a state of blissful intoxication. Then she found out that he was having sexual relations with a number of other women patients, and that was the first time she thought he might have been intentionally exploiting and deceiving her. She confided her thoughts to Barbara, a fellow patient, but Barbara went straight to the therapist and told him about their conversation. His response was to show Barbara Helga's confidential letters to him, describing them as the products of "psychotic" disturbances and coolly asserting that everything Helga had said was pure invention and the expression of her particular pathological condition. In fact, he said, things had been just the other way around: Helga had tried to seduce him and was now getting back at him because he had rejected her advances.

Toward Helga the therapist continued to uphold the image of an entirely sincere person with nothing to blame himself for, and she was only too eager to subscribe to that image. She had no former experience of an imposter operating on such an ambitious and accomplished scale, and rather than cast aspersions on his character she preferred to doubt herself, her common sense, and her memory. At first, Barbara had been indignant when Helga told her of the sexual exploitation, but now she was completely transformed, refused to believe her, and called her a liar to her face. Helga racked her brains to find a reason for this change. It never occurred to her that the therapist might have given Barbara a loaded version of what had happened.

Helga's therapist now indicated his readiness to "guide her through" this "phase" and treat her for her "paranoid visions." In the process, he did everything he could to wipe out or place a different interpretation on memories of any sexual encounters between them. For a time she was touched by his caring attitude. But when he openly threatened her with hospitalization and litigation if she ever told anyone about her "fantasies," she suddenly started suspecting that it might not be the first time he was dealing with a situation like this. Only now did she remember her phone conversation with his wife and realize that she had been trying to warn her. This man was obviously well-versed in the art of intimidation. The penny had taken a long time to drop, but it was not too late. Without this knowledge, Helga would have gone on submitting herself to his brainwashing. Instead, she broke off all contact with her therapist. It took a long time for her to free herself of the emotional confusion and the severe physical symptoms that were its aftermath. It was Brigit, a social worker and therapist with years of experience working with incestuous families, who helped her to come to terms with the harm that her therapist had inflicted on her.

Today, Helga feels that the main reason this man succeeded in reducing his patients to such an abject state of submission was that he agreed to give therapy only to people who were easy to intimidate and confuse. In most cases, the victims of his brainwashing would never be able to extricate themselves from the effects of it. If she hadn't been through it herself, she would never have believed that such emotional bondage was still possible in this day and age. In her perplexity, she tried to reestablish contact with Barbara, but again everything she had to say fell on deaf ears. She had the feeling that Barbara was not allowing herself to so much as countenance any idea that her therapist had not previously vetted and approved. She was appalled at this kind of mental subjugation and glad that she could tell Brigit about it.

"I'm sure you know," Brigit said despondently, "that a manipulated brain registers the harm done to it as if it were a boon, sometimes until it's too late to get out of the trap at all. Okay, your example shows that it is possible to extricate yourself. But it also shows that there are therapists who are so clever at disclaiming

their involvements with patients that they're willing to risk
making those women lose their minds. For a thoroughly nasty,
calculating therapist, that is in fact not a risk; it's a reassurance.
After all, no court of law will give credence to statements from
a person who's psychotic."

Helga was not content to be indignant and just leave it at
that. Her own experience prevented her from looking down on
other women's credulity, let alone making light of it. But she also
wanted to use that experience to get a clearer picture of what it
was that had so persistently kept her from sizing up the situation
she was in.

While she was going through her therapy with Brigit, Helga
remet her best friend Michelle in Santa Barbara. Michelle had
been living in Peru for six years, and Helga had not seen her
since she left. She gave her the bare bones of what her therapist
had done to her, but she was still suffering from the shock and
was not able to confide in her friend completely. She promised
to write to her. But it was Michelle who wrote first.

DEAR HELGA,

When we met in Santa Barbara, you said you'd be writing
and telling me what you've been through these last six years, but
so far I haven't heard from you. That was six months ago, and
I'm writing because I want to make sure that we don't lose
touch again. When I went to Peru six years ago, I missed you a
lot. Then I immersed myself in my work and got used to not
having a friend as close as you always were. I tried to keep in
touch, but your replies were few and far between, and also
rather distant and noncommittal. I couldn't explain this coolness
that had come between us. I just assumed that you were either
mad at me for going away, or that you had other, closer friends.

So I never asked you what was behind it all. (But that's when you met your therapist.) Although you've now seen through him and have found Brigit, you still don't seem to me entirely free of his influence. That's the impression I got, anyway. In everything you said I could sense your relief at having freed yourself from the clutches of that charlatan, but at the same time you seemed troubled about how you could have got into that situation in the first place. It was like you still didn't dare to feel the full impact of your rage and indignation. You were very controlled and told me all those horrible things with no outward signs of agitation, and sometimes you even laughed. To tell you the truth, I couldn't help feeling that there was a part of you that still hadn't really engaged with them. You told me about the whole thing as if you were quite remote from the person it had happened to.

I didn't want to pressure you; I thought maybe it was too early for you to come to terms with this trauma. How are you doing now? I'd love to talk to you, but I'm going to wait until you want us to meet. We always used to get along so well, and I can't see why it shouldn't stay that way. If you can, write and tell me what you think.

All my love,
MICHELLE

DEAR MICHELLE,

Forgive me for not having written sooner. I didn't forget my promise, but I needed those six months to get things clear in my mind. Now I think I've managed that, and I would have been in touch soon even if you hadn't written first. Well, this is going to be a pretty long letter, so brace yourself!

Where do I start? You know how much you've always meant to me, how important your friendship was to me. There was nobody who understood me better, nobody so ready to accept me just as I was. You know how completely I trusted you, how much I treasured your straightforwardness and honesty.

Six years ago you went to live in Peru. For me it was as if you had died. You were still out there somewhere, and I could always have written. All I needed to do to keep up the contact was to answer all your wonderful, affectionate letters. But I couldn't. Of course, I dashed off a few friendly lines now and again, but what I really felt was that you had gone for good. It took me a long time to realize that.

It wasn't until after we met six months ago that I found the key that I had been looking for throughout that whole incident with the therapist. The first thing was that Brigit suddenly realized that she hardly knew anything about you. She asked me to tell her what it was like when you left six years ago, what I felt about it, and what I had said to you. Do you know what? I couldn't remember! And that really shook me. She said: "Isn't that strange? Your best friend goes all that way away and you have no memory of saying good-bye? Did you feel left all high and dry after she'd gone?"

"No," I said, "I didn't feel anything at all." I said those words quite calmly, astonished at my own coolness. But at the same time I noticed that I felt somehow defiant, like a child whose feelings are hurt and won't let anyone get near her. How come? I asked myself. Brigit is good to me; she's trying to help me. I have no reason to turn a deaf ear when she asks me something. As soon as I thought that, my defiance broke down altogether. I don't know why, but I suddenly burst out crying. I felt the pain of being abandoned, a pain that I had refused to feel when you went away. I had pushed it to one side because I felt it was somehow not relevant. But now I finally realized just how relevant it actually was.

You know my father died when I was four. I was left alone with my mother, who had all kinds of problems herself and wasn't able to give me any feeling of security or protection. She kept me on a pretty tight leash, but at the same time she was clinging and possessive because she needed someone, and there was no one there except me. In her presence, how could I have felt, let alone shown, the sorrow and despair I felt at the loss of my father? It was impossible in the situation I was in. Above all else my mother expected self-control. The last thing she wanted was any show of feelings, particularly as she was jealous of my love for my father. So my feelings had to stay underground. From one day to the next, I had to accept that my father, who had always loved me, was gone forever, and that I was expected to live with that fact, not doing, saying, or feeling a thing.

And when you went away, it was the same pattern. I couldn't cry. It was as if someone had told me not to, and in a sense I consigned you to the grave, there and then. The worst thing was that I was still searching for my father, like a little child. What does a four-year-old know about death, about irrevocable loss? My mother took every opportunity she could to drum good manners into me. Maybe I believed my father would come back if I behaved myself? Or perhaps I was trying to die a little myself, killing my feelings so as to be closer to him. I don't know. I have no memory at all of what I thought at the time. All I know is that no one took the trouble to talk to me about my loss, to explain things to me or comfort me. Good manners were expected of me, but no questions. So I got used to not asking any.

Shortly after you went away, I fell in love with Paul. I got pregnant, but he was against me having the baby, and he left me

a little later. So the father of my child was gone before that
child had to suffer the consequences of an unhappy marriage.
I stayed behind with Flora, still doing my best to see things as
level-headedly as possible. Luckily I found a baby-sitter for her,
a cousin of mine. I started working again, ignored my distress,
persuaded myself I was just "nervous," went to see problem
families, did what I could for neglected children. Outwardly,
everything was fine. The immense inner pressure I was under
came out in the form of chronic insomnia. I had to take more
and more sleeping pills, and it was then that I realized I needed
help.

I decided to embark on that therapy I've told you so much
about. It was supposed to help me to get in touch with my
childhood feelings and cope with them that way. That was what
I was hoping for. But in reality I still felt the same permanent,
infantile helplessness and the impotent, raging anger that came
with it, and had no idea what could conceivably bring it all to
an end. I cried a lot, but I wasn't able to get any benefit from it.
I spent years in that state. The only one to get anything out of it
was the therapist.

I didn't have much money of my own, but after my mother
died, my parents' big house in Palm Springs was all mine. The
mortgage had been paid off, so I was able to borrow money
from the bank to pay the high therapy fees. It was the therapist
who suggested this to me, right at the beginning. The initial fee
of $100 per hour rose in the course of time to $250. I was never
asked for my consent. There was this tacit assumption that I
would pay up and not make a fuss. After all, I was a wealthy
home owner and I could afford it quite easily. The therapist
talked me into decisions and expenditures that brought him all
kinds of advantages and did me nothing but harm. But that
permanent weeping in his presence put me on the level of a

little girl unable to see what other people are doing with her. He profited from my idealizing transference instead of breaking it down. It was a vicious circle I just couldn't get out of.

Another thing he did was to systematically denigrate all the people I was in any way close to—you, my colleagues at work, my cousins—until in the end he was the only person I had left. He was getting such good mileage out of my positive father transference that he really saw no reason to help me, even if he had had the therapeutic skill it would have taken to do so. But he didn't. The only technique he had mastered was to encourage people's insatiable infantile needs until they couldn't stand it any longer and then hold out the prospect of relief from their condition, promising that he had the remedy for their sufferings. And to achieve that relief, people are willing to submit to all kinds of exploitation—financial, emotional, and sexual.

Sexual abuse frequently plays a central role; the humiliation the women are subjected to and the sham intimacy that kind of relationship establishes are designed to prevent them from seeing through their exploiters. I was seeking my father in this therapist and allowed myself to be seduced and manipulated by him without noticing what was going on because, come what may, I was trying to keep my father alive in my transference. In line with the scenario of my childhood, what I feared most was my father's death, that death which had deprived me of love and left me exposed to the power my mother had over me.

But it was precisely what I so badly wanted to prevent that finally happened. The idealization of my father was not the only thing that kept me shackled to that man. I was now in a state of dependency on someone who made me believe he was willing and able to help me and who didn't have the slightest scruples about maneuvering me into a psychotic state to cover up what he had done. It was something my mother used to do as well, telling me I hadn't really experienced what I thought I'd experienced, and plunging me into a state of profound uncertainty and insecurity. I was so used to it that there was no chance of my realizing that my therapist was doing exactly the same. Except that he did it much more systematically and skillfully.

It wasn't till I met Brigit that I figured this all out. Just imagine, within a few months she had helped to understand why I had let myself be blinded by that man for so long. He managed to make me believe in his healing powers; he even showed me written testimonies, letters from people he had "cured." Later it turned out they were all fakes. Emotionally, I was still the little daughter meekly putting up with her mother's treatment in the hope of "deserving" the return of her father, who in her imagination had never really died. And then I fell into the clutches of a man who specialized in making optimum use of the specific distress of his patients. What gave him his power over me was the grief I had disavowed so early and the defense against my old helplessness, which he reawakened in my adult self and then cultivated and exploited in so many ways.

When we met six months ago, I couldn't have told you all this. It was only after you came back that I finally got in touch with my sorrow at my father's death. I can't tell you how glad I am that you came back and helped me to finally understand my story, just by being there. And how glad I am to have been able to write this letter.

All my love,
HELGA

DEAR HELGA,

I'm glad, too, glad that you were able to write and tell me the whole story, and glad and grateful that you wanted to confide in me. Now I can hear your real voice again. I can hear you speaking with your own words and being frank and open the way you used to be. The last time we met I still had this unnerving feeling that there was some kind of veil between us. I sensed your reserve, sensed that you were wary, cagey in a way you'd never been before. No wonder. After those terrible experiences you were bound to be suspicious of everything and everyone, myself included. When someone who's been promised help, sympathy, and recovery comes up against lies and deceit, how can they possibly have a trusting attitude to others? I could tell that from the way you were talking. You used to express yourself so naturally, with so much sensitivity; you used to be open and straightforward, just like you were in your last letter. And suddenly there you were trotting out all those expressions that seemed so stereotyped, so lifeless. It was this, among other things, that told me that your therapist (you never mentioned his name; it was as if you found it so repulsive you couldn't bring yourself to pronounce it) had a great deal in common with all those other gurus that are springing up all over the world these days.

As you know, I've been doing a lot of work recently on sects. It was Carol L. Mithers's[1] book that put me on to it, a book describing the birth and growth of a sect in the seventies. I'd like to tell you about it so that you can see that you're not the only one whose personal need has been exploited for others' gain. The gurus are no less in need than their victims, of course; it's just that they refuse to see it. They put on a show for their victims and bask in their admiration. Did you ever hear of the "feeling therapy" that was all the rage back home twenty-five years ago? You were still a child then, and I was a teenager with no interest in the therapy scene. A short while back, I heard some things you should know because some of them at least mirror so exactly what you've been through yourself.

In the late sixties, lots of young people were fascinated by Arthur Janov's book *The Primal Scream*. The book contained reports by patients who had freed themselves of their symptoms by reliving repressed childhood feelings in therapy. After the book appeared, Janov was approached for help by thousands of people, and of course he couldn't take them all on as patients. Then, in 1970, it looked as if there was an alternative for all those people who had drawn a blank with him. Two young psychologists who had trained very briefly at Janov's Institute of Primal Therapy opened a center of their own in Los Angeles. They called it "feeling therapy." Both of them had a degree in psychology and they were supported and recommended by famous psychologists like Carl Rogers and Eugene Gendlin. Their declared aim was to provide a less authoritarian version of primal therapy than they felt Arthur Janov did. They did, however, adopt the initial intensive three-week period leading to the sudden disintegration of the patients' defense structures and to extreme regression and dependency on the therapist. In pursuing this course, they created power structures to which they themselves finally fell victim.

The therapy group numbered some two hundred persons, and it soon turned into a cult-type community like so many other groups of that kind. They cut themselves off from the outside world and recruited new members. After going through the intensive period and the subsequent "therapy," these new-comers were quickly transformed into fervent adherents. The center flourished. They opened branches in Boston, Montreal, and Hawaii, and the founders advanced to the status of media personalities. In numerous interviews, they were adamant that their theory would enable them to turn the world into a paradise full of emotive, peaceable, responsible people. The demand for the therapy they were offering skyrocketed, and their prosperity grew accordingly.

Among the new applicants for admittance to "total health" via feeling therapy were a number of company owners. Once accepted as patients, they were expected to make generous donations and ended up handing over their flower shops and car repair companies to the center, subsequently working there as employees from five in the morning till late at night for a salary of $400 to $600 a month. After they finished work, they were required to attend group sessions at which they were allegedly given therapy. In reality, they were browbeaten and vilified for their "bad behavior" and had injunctions imposed on them which they had to fulfill within a given period. For example, married couples who loved each other "too much" were forced to have sex once an hour until they had finally had enough of each other and were ready to devote themselves single-mindedly and wholeheartedly to the group and to their work. On the other hand, people who didn't like each other were forced to have intimate relations. The terrible thing is that nobody opposed these perverted orders. The patients were understandably looking to their therapists for help and salvation, and they were occasionally given just enough personal attention to keep those expectations alive.

This mixture of pseudo-caring and covert exploitation was familiar to the patients from their own childhoods, and so they put up no resistance. That's why this docility training worked so well. In the end, the annual revenue coming into the center totalled several million dollars, enabling a small privileged group

to live in luxury and buy a ranch, while the "people"—a syn-
onym for a modern brand of slave—labored until they dropped
from exhaustion.

Although one of the founders left the community after a
few years, he did nothing to open the members' eyes. Word-
lessly, he discontinued his dealings with the therapy center, and
no one ever asked why. It was as if the members were all under
mass hypnosis.

Most of the members came from middle-class backgrounds.
They were intelligent people, many of them college graduates
accustomed to using their brains. But apparently no one ever
broke ranks. It was this that prompted me to take an interest in
sects and read more about them. I wanted to understand why, in
this day and age, people should willingly connive at their own
enslavement and bondage. It appears to be the regression into
infant helplessness that makes the patients either lose their critical faculties altogether or turn them against themselves.

Nine years later, a chance discovery revealed that the guru
had used all the donations from the members to run his ranch.
When the victims realized that the money they had contributed
in good faith had been plowed into his adolescent dreams of a
life on the range, all hell broke loose. In the hermetically sealed-
off therapy center a window had been opened, letting in light
and fresh air, and all thanks to the incontrovertible evidence of
bank statements. The whole thing collapsed like a house of
cards.

At last, suspicions systematically suppressed for nine years
were able to find a voice. All at once, the brainwashed patients
were confronted with reality. Years before, they had come to the
center to learn to feel, but they had been ruthlessly cut off from
their true feelings, because the last thing their therapists wanted
was emotional awareness on the part of their victims. The mem-

bers of the center now saw that they had been constantly
encouraged to level harsh criticism at their parents and at the
same time been deviously prevented from seeing through the
people who were exploiting and tormenting them. Suddenly
they were aware of having recounted the most intimate details
of their childhood and sex lives at their group sessions, while at
the same time burying deep inside themselves their true feelings
and thoughts about the behavior of the guru. There had been
no exchanges between group members. Strict regimentation of
the patients had seen to that. Pregnant members were forced to
have abortions, while sleep deprivation, bizarre dietary regula-
tions, and humiliating punishments were the order of the day.

The legal proceedings against the seven leading therapists
took four years. All except one denied having done anything
wrong, insisting that they had never damaged anyone, even
though in some cases they had had to resort to strict "measures"
in order to "protect the patients from themselves." They retali-
ated with lawsuits for defamation of character but lost on all
counts. Finally they lost their licenses to practice psychotherapy.
The patients were awarded compensation, substantial amounts
in many cases, but of course that did nothing to alleviate the
effects of the indoctrination they had been through. To get over
that, many of them had to spend years undergoing further therapy, this time of a reputable kind.

These alarming developments are not restricted to Los Angeles. You find them all over the world. This illustrates the huge
dangers and weaknesses of regressive forms of therapy. A person
suddenly thrust back into infantile dependency is completely
unable to integrate childhood experiences. That is something
that can only be done from the vantage of adulthood and with
the help of a therapist bolstering the patient's autonomy instead
of purposely keeping him in a state of infantile dependency. This

dependency is the fertile soil nurturing the illusion that the guru can give an adult person everything that she did not get from the mother: mirroring, understanding, unconditional affection. A mother with a strong bond with her child from the outset can give her this total fulfillment. But expecting a guru to be able to make up for those deficits is deceptive. All it leads to is a dependency on promises that can never be redeemed, because the member of a sect is not a newborn infant and the guru is not his mother. But this illusion is actively nurtured in many sects and religions.

The transformation of a therapy group into a cult in which the emotional lives of the members are kept under minute surveillance day in day out, may seem at first glance some sort of horror story from a B-movie. But the devastating development of "feeling therapy" is well-documented and reflects a phenomenon that is only too familiar to experts on the way sects work.

Maybe all this will be some comfort to you if you know you're not the only one to have been through this kind of thing and that others have managed to extricate themselves from the chaos that resulted.

All my love,
MICHELLE

DEAR MICHELLE,

Thank you for your letter. I thought I had got over my feelings of indignation, but that certainly fanned the flames again! Of course, I've always known that I wasn't the only one, and I know only too well from my own personal experience how indoctrination can undermine and break down your personality once you start believing in it. When I first suspected that I might have fallen into the hands of a fraud, I went in search of other people who had been in contact with him. They told me things that made me sick to my stomach, but the odd thing was they didn't seem much affected by them at all. I got in touch with Barbara, but she was unwilling to listen to a single idea that didn't come directly from him. I had the impression that the sentences coming out of her mouth hadn't taken shape in her own brain. It was really frightening. Maybe that's the way I seemed to you six months ago. When I think back to my encounter with Barbara, it still gives me the creeps.

But it wasn't all traumatic. There were good things, as well. I met a small number of women who like myself had escaped from the harem and found people to help them. One of them was Laura. We talked things over together and realized that this man not only had exploited us sexually but had actually made money out of his perverted activities as well. He had encouraged me to write about certain subjects, drug problems, teenage dropouts, that kind of thing. He showed Laura a slightly doctored-up version of these articles, passing them off to her as his own. He did exactly the same with Laura's articles on certain syndromes, showing them to me as if he had written them himself. That way he gained our confidence in his powers and made us admire him for his wide-ranging interests.

That in itself would have been just harmless vanity, a minor deception. But he took it a stage further. He actually made me pay him by the hour for reading my stuff, and in the end the money I was shelling out ran into thousands. He did the same thing with Laura who he also knew had plenty of money. By the way, when I told Barbara all this she wasn't in the least bothered by it. She said that he didn't use the money for himself but for "the cause," and that he gave loans to people who didn't have my kind of money but who needed to come to him for therapy. In fact, it was true that he didn't accept only rich patients. He offered the others huge loans that they paid off by working for him for nothing. But as the therapy never came to an end, they were always in arrears. And that made them terminally dependent on him. Most of them mutated into mindless mouthpieces, spouting his doctrine, singing his praises, and never realizing that they had become minions, personal property, objects he had acquired at rock-bottom prices.

I still remember the faint misgivings I felt when I got his exorbitant bills, but I ignored them. After all, what did the money matter compared to the fact that someone was taking my ideas and suggestions seriously and helping me to get them published? I don't mind telling you that for a time I offered him money of my own accord, thinking that he was really interested in my work in the social services and my ideas on how the system could be reformed.

When I was a teenager, about fifteen, I wrote poems and short stories. No one in the family took any interest in them. My mother said it was all nonsense and a waste of time, although she didn't know what they were about, never having the time to read them when I asked her to. On one occasion she made fun of them to a cousin of mine, and after that I stopped trying to get anyone to read them. I was too afraid of being misunderstood, and I didn't want people making sarcastic remarks about them. For a long time, I wrote in secret. I didn't even let you in on it. But it was awful for me not to be able to share my poetry with anyone.

When my therapist offered to read my articles closely and tell me what he thought of them, I was happy and grateful. Money was no object. In my infantile state of mind I never realized that some day I was going to have to pay back the loan and the interest out of my earnings. My dearest wish—one

never fulfilled in my childhood—was to find someone to share
my interests and my enthusiasms. But eventually I was to realize
that my therapist's interest in social issues was a hoax. All he
wanted was to get as much profit as he could out of my present
situation and the hang-ups I was dragging around with me. And
he succeeded in all kinds of ways.

It took a good long talk between Laura and me to make us
fully aware of the humiliation involved in paying him that
money. It was a devaluation of what we had produced, like
admitting that reading our work was a chore and a nuisance for
him, whereas in fact he was profiting from it. And not only
financially. It was a source of useful new information for him, as
well. He never showed any appreciation for the other things I
did for him either. In that relationship there was a built-in
inequality that I never questioned because I saw my therapist as
I had seen my mother, from the perspective of a child willing to
do anything without expecting anything in return.

I imagine you'll want to know what it was exactly that I did
for him. The details will remind you of the sect you told me
about in Los Angeles. In my case, there was a whole range of
things I was expected to do, all of them taking an immense
amount of time and energy. I was responsible for dealing with
his correspondence, organizing his filing system, modernizing
the office organization, doing translation work, and lots of other
things besides.

Then there were these therapy sessions with three chronically ill women whose physical disabilities made them unable to
leave the house. At the time I never suspected they were former
victims of his miracle cures whose state he was doing his best to
keep under wraps. As a social worker, I had experience with
home care, so he suggested it would be good for my personal
development to do something for other people without being

paid for it. It wasn't until later that I learned he had been charg-
ing these women a fee for my services.

The humiliation I felt when I found that out was crippling. I
felt so incredibly dumb when I realized all the things I had let
myself be talked into in pursuit of the fulfillment of my infantile
wishes. I was so ashamed of my stupidity I never told anyone
about it, thinking they were bound to ask how I could be such
a fool. But I wasn't afraid to tell you. After what you told me
about the way "feeling therapy" worked, I knew you wouldn't
look down on me because you understand the mechanisms; you
know how these people operate.

I think lots of people are ashamed of having let themselves
be exploited. And this false shame keeps them in a state of victimization. That's what stops people who manage to escape
from these sects from reporting clearly and in detail exactly how
they have been deceived. If they do decide to go public, what
they say is frequently so vague that no court of law can make
much of it. It is the shame of the victims that enables the perpetrators to get off scot-free and carry on with their fraudulent
activities. Once I realized that, I did everything I could not to
forget what had happened to me but to understand it in all its
aspects.

After that meeting with Laura I still hadn't achieved the
inner stability I have now. But there was one thing I managed to
do, and looking back, I'm glad I did it. I sent him a bill for services rendered. I knew he'd never pay it. I knew he'd just ignore
it, and that's precisely what happened. But I owed it to myself,
to my own sense of dignity, to list what I had done and to give
it a value. Making out that bill was like saying, I have a right to
be paid. I'm no longer a child that anyone can use and make a
fool of.

Writing that bill also put an end to the pattern I'd been

living. I had understood that although the mental aftereffects
of a tragic childhood are likely to lead to chronic lack of self-
esteem, we can still get over those emotional lesions when we
grow up. Realizing that is the first step toward breaking with
the compulsion to repeat. We recognize that we were abused
children, patients, guru-worshippers, and that recognition gives
us the freedom to leave it all behind us.

Gurus and all those other little tin gods can never take that
step. They have to stay up on their pedestal, whatever the cost.
They steadfastly deny that they were ever victims, and escape
into power games, promises of salvation, roles, posturing, dis-
sembling, and often enough fraud and embezzlement. They too
are trying in their own way to extricate themselves from the
crippling legacy of their childhood, but all they achieve is an
illusion of inner liberation, and only at other people's expense.
Deep down, they are repeating what their parents did to them,
often in a much more extreme way. A conscious survivor of
abuse will not seek salvation in controlling and manipulating
others.

One thing that I felt really bad about for a long time was
that I recommended this therapist to two of my colleagues at
work. At the time I believed in his integrity, the way they
believe in him today. I now know that tragically there are
women in this man's "sect" who have been trapped there for
years without achieving the slightest awareness of it. His adherents, admirers, and victims choose what their own biographies
let them or make them choose. I stopped feeling responsible for
their future when I realized that they didn't want to be rescued.

Realizing that was what enabled me to stop trying the
impossible. I'm not alone anymore, I have Brigit and now I have
you. I want to thank you just for being there and writing to me,
helping me to show you my feelings, to stop burrowing down

into my own loneliness, to trust people who have my real interests at heart. As a child I had no option, no alternative to my
loneliness. But now I do. I was able to help myself as soon as I
was willing to look things in the face. It's interesting that in all
those years of so-called therapy, I always got an ophthalmic
migraine when I forced myself to tolerate my therapist's behavior and to suppress my feelings of instinctive repulsion. As soon
as I faced up to the truth, that symptom disappeared and never
came back.

All my love,
HELGA

DEAR HELGA,

Your last letter gave me plenty to think about. It made me
realize that we often tend to dwell on financial things because
they're more factual. We get all worked up about them because
it's the kind of exploitation you can prove and that other people
are more likely to be able to understand. The whole "feeling
therapy" business is a case in point. But what you describe goes
much deeper. In your attempt to find out what that exploitation
has meant for your emotional life, you made a discovery that
was of course a very personal one but, at the same time, is
something that lots of survivors and mistreated children have
been through: the humiliation, the depreciation that perpetuates
itself and makes so many children unable to have any idea of
their own value when they grow up.

To compensate for that, adults will choose some other way
of acquiring the value they have been persuaded they don't
intrinsically have, either by taking advantage of others or by
becoming overachievers, stepping up their self-imposed stan-

dards of excellence all the time because they have no gauge to assess themselves by. I don't know what it is that makes some choose the destructive option while others go for the self-destructive alternative, but I'm convinced that you're right in what you say. Only by facing up to the fact that we were victims do we have any chance of opting out of the exploiter-victim spiral and giving up both roles.

If your therapist had been able to grasp what he was doing, if he'd been able to admit as much to his victims, it would have opened up the path to a new life for him. But his involvements with his victims seem to have gone back a long way, and the slightest concession would have meant the risk of bringing down an avalanche of lawsuits from people suddenly given leave to see through him. Understandably, it's not a risk he's likely to take. So he'll go on capitalizing on other people's weaknesses, psychiatrizing his critics, and probably maximizing his profits as long as there's a demand for gurus.

That demand doesn't look as if it's going to die out for a long time yet. There are many people who have never experienced love and who are therefore incapable of seeing how they are being double-crossed by their gurus. The fact that you were ultimately able to do so may have something to do with those few experiences of love you had, the love your aunt and your father gave you. People whose childhood is marked by the total absence of any kind of affection will hardly be able to grasp, let alone identify with, the conclusions you've come to. As your mother's child, you suffered terribly from the suppression and negation of your personality, but at least you weren't exposed to physical cruelty. Your mental distress drove you into the clutches of an emotional vampire, but there was something in your earlier life that gave you a chance to finally get away from him. There are probably

very many people who were never given that chance when
they were children. And that means their chances of breaking
free of a sect are very low.

What you say supports my own conviction that it is of
immeasurable value for a therapy victim to know someone
who can confirm her observations. That will help her to get
over the worst of it. Whether that happens in therapy, with
people she knows, or through counseling is ultimately immate-
rial. All that counts is for a person to be able to tell someone
else what has happened to them instead of being encouraged
to seek the source of their troubles in their parents alone.
Because the only way you can work through the situation is in
the here and now. A child cannot do that. In my work in Peru
I've made a number of interesting observations I'd like to tell
you about when we meet. The Indians I work with are astonishingly receptive to ideas that in our culture still encounter
the most stubborn resistance. In my own professional environment among the social workers here, I frequently come up
against views I consider outdated. That's why I'm so glad we
get along the way we do.

The experience I have gathered in the last few years has
taught me that the aftereffects of a childhood trauma can be
overcome by getting rid of the actual trauma. As you describe it,
those aftereffects take the form of an anxiety-induced blockage;
they make you speechless, chronically depressed, and disconso-
late. I agree with you. Once an adult has got over that anxiety,
he has no need to sink back into the old helplessness, despair,
and silence. The impotent rage of the child will probably only
reassert itself if the adult voluntarily relapses into the kind of
dependency he had no choice but to live in as a child. That was
why all that crying in the presence of your therapist did nothing
to help you find a way out. The way out was barred, just as it

was in your childhood. Your regression to the state of an infant made it impossible for you to see that someone was quite simply making money out of your tears.

Children have no way of finding witnesses for the wrongs done to them. If they're unlucky, they will be left completely alone with their distress. They can turn to other members of the family, but relatives are frequently reluctant to side with a child against the parents. An adult, on the other hand, has all kinds of opportunities for finding the right listener. It has long been proven that a shock is best overcome not by trying to forget it, the way we used to be told, but by talking about it and feeling what it meant to us until the shock starts losing its significance. Silence is the worst enemy of people who have been harmed that way.

It's no coincidence that Freud regarded the paralytic phenomena of his first hysterical patients as an expression of enforced silence. Women frequently express their inner state via physical symptoms, displaying bouts of paralysis and language dysfunctions precisely circumscribing their mental distress. It's as if they were saying, "I must keep silence. I mustn't show my rage, not even recognize who makes me so angry. I must believe what people tell me. I mustn't betray anyone. I must stay motionless until my rage kills me." I know of women who became physically ill because they couldn't bring themselves to file a lawsuit for the sexual exploitation they underwent in therapy. When it was finally too late for litigation, their last resort was to fall ill.

What makes this anxiety about speaking out so persistent is the fact that it has its roots in childhood. But it cannot be overcome by lapsing back into a state of infancy. It has to be faced up to in the here and now. Good group therapy can be helpful. For many children, breaking their silence means literally risking their lives. For adults, that is only the case in totalitarian regimes, and many sects fully live up to that definition. They are based on the old education system that is all too familiar to people who have been swallowed up by sects and cult groups because it is the way they were brought up themselves. Some therapies work on the same principle. The therapist interprets criticisms from his patients as transferences, thus denying them any substance from the outset. As you know, the minds of the patients are subjected to such massive manipulation that in the end they no longer have the courage to trust their own perceptions, and finally come to actively fear them.

Though this mental manipulation can have a devastating effect on the mind, it will not necessarily affect the body. But there are other kinds of manipulation, for instance, the emotional kind, that, unlike the mental variety, are extremely quick to have an effect on the body. To my mind, this is what miracle cures thrive on. There are people with so-called charisma (shamans are an example), a talent for emotional manipulation. Depending on their ethical principles and personal interests, some use this talent to help other people; others to undo them. When charisma is coupled with a pathological desire for recognition and a psychopathic character, the person in question is all set to embark on a career of devastating destruction. This was obviously the case with your therapist. But he's not the only one. There's a whole group of such people, and it's growing all the time.

A survey in the United States[2] has shown that 30 percent of practicing therapists have never themselves consulted a therapist, which means they have never questioned their own motives.

Of course, there are still the reputable therapists who proceed with the greatest circumspection in uncovering the wounds of their patients and thus help them to integrate their

feelings. But more and more charlatans are trying to make
money out of induced regression. The initial euphoria of these
sorcerers' apprentices doesn't usually last very long. As time goes
on, unruly transferences and countertransferences materialize,
which they have never learned to handle. The therapist may be
able to hold the patient in check for a while with indoctrination and manipulation. But even the perverted pleasures of sexual exploitation will only temporarily outweigh the serious
trouble he will have in dealing with unexpected crises and real
emergencies.

There's no way of putting a stop to these people and their
dealings because there's obviously a "demand" for their services,
even if that demand is likely to be self-destructive. All we can do
is identify the operative mechanisms. But as long as people are
willing to connive at their own deception, the gurus will go on
doing a roaring trade. Many of the people who came under the
influence of famous cult leaders in the seventies have long since
set themselves up as gurus in their own right. And the whole
thing is spiraling because the profound emotional disturbances
inflicted on the victims drive a number of them to start exploiting others in their turn.

There are therapy designs that are such a confusing mixture of good things and bad things that it's almost impossible
for psychological laypersons to form an accurate judgment
about them. For me, it is undeniable that working through
one's childhood is an essential part of therapy. However, the
promise of total cure by means of rituals and intensive regression can involve patients in a futile lifelong effort that is
dangerously addictive. But you don't need me to tell you
that.

The things you've been through are familiar to me from my
reading and my own work. The conclusions we come to are

very much the same. We'll have a lot more to talk about when
we meet, and I'm really looking forward to it!

Take care, Helga, and enjoy the freedom you've finally
achieved for yourself!

All my love,
MICHELLE

GLORIA

Wisdom from the Heart

NANCY AND LOUISE STUDIED sociology together at Princeton. After graduating, Louise married a businessman, had four daughters, and lived with her family in a big house in Rowayton, Connecticut. Nancy obtained a teaching position at the University of San Francisco. She found her research work fascinating, and in California she met people whose ideas and outlook on life were more congenial to her than the people she knew from New Jersey.

In the first few years the two former fellow students called each other occasionally, but as time went by the miles between them and the changes in their lifestyles caused them to drift apart. Louise became a Junior Leaguer, while Nancy devoted her energies more and more to the women's movement. When

Nancy finally married and had a child with Down's syndrome, all contact between them broke off. This was not because Louise had stopped caring but more the result of a strange, inhibiting feeling of not knowing what to do or say.

Louise felt awkward about calling Nancy up out of the blue and asking her how things were going. And the longer she put it off, the more difficult it got. She told herself that her friend would probably prefer to be left alone. Or was that just an excuse? Wasn't she avoiding getting in touch for fear of hearing an account of a personal destiny that she didn't know how to respond to? She was not clear in her mind whether it was her friend's feelings she was concerned to spare or her own. But she did nothing to find out. That way forty years went by.

Today, Louise is a grandmother of long standing, and her grandchildren give her great joy. But recently, her eldest daughter gave birth to a baby with Down's syndrome, although the condition could have been diagnosed early and then she could have had an abortion. The decision to have her baby without any prenatal checkups was a conscious one, and her daughter is standing up to this situation with rather more fortitude and equanimity than her parents. It occurs to Louise that now might be the time to reestablish contact with Nancy. She no longer needs to spare her friend's feelings or keep her distance. The new situation has broken down the barriers between them, and she genuinely wants to see her old friend again. Nancy is looking forward to their reunion. Her husband died some time back, and her daughter is living in a nursing home. As she has no other children, she is a free agent and can take the time to answer her friend's questions as best she can. And so they finally find themselves sitting opposite each other, trying to give a reasonably cogent account of the most important events in their lives.

Louise tells her friend how successful her daughters have

been, college graduates all of them and all with their own families. She talks about her grandchildren and her husband and how
the two of them still get along as well as they always have. Nancy
makes no bones about the fact that she, too, would love to have
grandchildren. But she feels no resentment. She likes Louise and
is happy for her. She herself has always differed from the main-
stream middle-class ideas about what a woman's life should look
like. Maybe, she thinks to herself, maybe I wouldn't have been
much good as a grandmother.

"You're different from what I was expecting," Louise says. "I
had this vision of you as the mother of a disabled child, all em-
bittered and ravaged. I remember you never used to do things
the easy way, even when you were a student. But you seem vital
and relaxed. What was it like for you when Gloria was born? Did
you have good friends here in California? Did they rally round
you? Did your husband stand by you? How did he see the whole
thing?"

"He was completely helpless and clammed up even more.
And my friends? I did think I had friends," says Nancy, "but all of
a sudden I was on my own. My best friend even advised me to
put Gloria in a home right away so that there wouldn't be any
bonds between us. That made me realize what a gulf there was
between us. She was totally insensitive to the fact that I already
loved my child more than anything else in my life. After the
birth, neither the obstetrician nor the pediatrician came out
with the truth, although they must have known. It was an obvious case of Down's syndrome. They kept me in the dark for days
and went on talking about what they 'suspected.'

"I still know exactly how I felt when they finally told me the
whole truth. I walked through the streets of San Francisco all
alone, thinking for the first time in my life, I'm up against something I can't escape and I can't do anything about. The problems

my parents had were something I could run away from. But I can't just leave this child to fend for herself, just give her away the way my friends suggested. You can't give your own heart away. As I say, I already loved the child. But I was also worried about my career, which was important to me.

"You'll probably remember that when I was a student, I always tried to do things the rational way. At home I had learned to keep my feelings under control, basically because I was scared of them. But later that strict self-surveillance, day in, day out, made it very difficult for me to get back in touch with my childhood, a period I really and truly knew next to nothing about. It was a complete blockage. Even psychoanalysis couldn't break it down completely.

"Only when Gloria was born did my feelings reawaken. She just took me by storm, and there was no going back. For the first time in my life I felt I was loved unconditionally. There was none of the fear I used to have of being exploited, taken advantage of, lied to. Once she was born, I didn't feel the need to run and hide.

"When I was a child, I had no one I could be really open with. I was the oldest daughter, so I got saddled with the responsibility for the others, and I was the one who got told off when they got up to mischief. It was only now, with my daughter, that I felt secure and trusting, feelings I'd never been able to develop as a child. At a very early age I had to play mother not only to my brothers and sisters but also to my parents, who never accepted any responsibility, either for what they did or what they said. That was why I wanted to consign my own youth to oblivion. At college that wasn't too much of a problem. But when I got married, my childhood caught up with me with a vengeance. Again, I was the person who had to be there for someone else to lean on, Richard this time. And I found it very hard to take.

"Gloria made it possible for me to learn to love her and to let that love grow. There were other people who wanted me to love them, but for various reasons there often came a point when they withdrew into themselves. They were not used to being shown affection. Gloria's not like that; she has no hang-ups about letting herself be loved. She drinks in every sign of affection and relishes it to the full. Quite simply, like a child. For me, that was even more of a gift than the love she gave me, because her love was bound to have something to do with her very real dependence on me. That still reminds me of the huge responsibilities I had to bear as a child."

"What was it like right at the beginning?"

"At the hospital, they told me she had a heart defect and they were keeping her on the neonatal ward to have the necessary tests done. I went along with that, of course. I had no idea at the time what would come of it. Today, I'd say: 'I'm taking her home with me; she needs her mother—breast-feeding won't do her heart any harm.' Her heart's just fine, by the way, always has been. Physically she's pretty sturdy. But that first unnecessary separation from me really left its mark. She has incredibly precise memories of those first few days, and in her drawings, the hospital ward turns up over and over again. She calls it the 'waiting room' because she spent all her time waiting for me to come back. She obviously suffered from being alone, and the medical equipment frightened her, as well. The pain of that separation keeps on coming back. Whenever she feels abandoned by someone she loves or when she finds herself in an environment that doesn't give her the explanations and information she needs to find her way about, she's very quick to think that she's been 'dumped,' that she's all alone in the world. That first separation knocked me off balance, too, but thanks to the breast-feeding, there was soon a deep sense of trust between us.

"As time went by, I got to know intuitively what she really needed, even if she couldn't say so herself. She got better at that, though, and I learned to understand her. I realized that for a long time I had assumed that things that were normal and natural to me must be just as obvious to her. But that wasn't the case, and she needed me to explain things to her much more often than I had imagined she would.

"It took me a long time to stop resenting the fact that fate had once again saddled me with the responsibility for another person, perpetuating a pattern I was trying to break now that I had understood it. Meanwhile I've learned a lot about Gloria. I see clearly that for certain practical things my daughter is dependent on other people's help and outside care. But emotionally she's amazingly self-assured. Her dependency imposes certain strains and restrictions on me, but she has also opened doors for me that had remained closed in my other relationships."

"How come?" Louise inquires. "Was it her helplessness? Did that awaken the feelings you'd been holding back?"

"No, it wasn't so much her helplessness, her obvious need: it was the trust she had in me, her ability to be open and genuine whatever the circumstances. That always touched me, and it helped me to become a little more open myself. She nearly always responds to affection with a demonstration of pleasure. And she doesn't bear anyone a grudge for being insensitive or indifferent. But lies she simply cannot stomach. She may not know the word for insincerity, but her body responds to it with severe physical symptoms: headaches, migraine, eczema. They usually go away again as soon as she has found words to say how she feels about the person in question. Gloria can't lie; she cannot hide her real self. She simply is as she is, totally honest and sincere. That's what makes it so easy to relate to her and to love her."

"And when did Gloria go into a home?"

"She lived with us for eighteen years. First she attended a privately run school for disabled children, and then we put her in a home. Gloria's teacher told us that the disabled need a protective, sheltering environment and that we should agree to the separation for her sake. We shouldn't bind ourselves to her too closely. At the time, her father and I fell in with the teacher's opinion and gave our consent. But I remember as if it was yesterday what I felt when we said good-bye, the pain of that separation. It was as if someone had torn a piece out of me, the dearest thing I had, as if they'd taken my love and destroyed it. I consoled myself, saying it was best for Gloria and that I'd soon come to terms with the situation, the way I always had. I longed to see her, of course, but the separation also gave me more freedom. Particularly after Richard died.

"Gloria spent thirteen years in that home. She seemed to like it; in fact, she seemed to be thriving on it. She came to me for the holidays, and any traveling I had to do I did in between times. It was only in 1987, while she was at home, that she told me she had seen a caretaker at the home holding an epileptic girl under the cold shower. As she spoke, I realized she had been living with fears she had been hiding from her own self. I wanted to extend the break for a while to work on those fears with her. But the administration of the home refused to comply. I for my part was not willing to send Gloria back there in such an apprehensive state of mind. The home responded by terminating the contract, and so she spent the next eight years living with me.

"Those were good years for both of us, really fulfilling. Gloria enjoyed gardening. When she planted flowers, she talked to the seedlings and wished them sturdy growth. She had to force herself to do any pruning because she was afraid of hurting the plants. But her greatest passion was dancing. She was completely uninhibited about improvising new steps and expressing her feelings that way. She took lessons, both group instruction and individual tuition, and took part in various performances. But as time wore on, she wanted to go back to some regular occupation. Finally, I found a new home with about thirty other disabled people. And that's where she lives now, working in the kitchen and the laundry."

"Didn't Gloria find it hard to acclimatize herself to a new home after being looked after by you all that time?" Louise asks.

"At first it was smooth sailing. Gloria is like a child in the sense that, when she does something, she wants to do it well and to other people's satisfaction, so that they'll praise her for it. It's just that she has much more experience and much greater awareness than a child. Also, she senses insincerity and has difficulty coming to terms with it. As far as I know, she has no problems with her job because she's good at what she does and she's also very conscientious. What sometimes gets in her way is her desire not to cause others any trouble. She's considerate and hates hurting people, so she tries to fall in with other people's moral value systems, even if they contradict her own sense of justice. Then she ignores her own feelings until they manifest themselves in the form of physical symptoms that are sometimes pretty persistent."

"What form does that take exactly?"

"I can give you a recent example. The theater group Gloria's in put on a performance in which she was cast as the mother. That was months ago. She had to hold an imaginary baby in her arms and sing it to sleep. Her dearest wish, which will sadly never come true, has always been to have a child of her own. Anyway, she spent months practicing this lullaby, but a few days before the performance she was told that the director had changed his mind. The cradle song had been cut and she was to

mime her role with dance steps, not saying a thing. Later, I found
out that singing, dancing, and speaking all together had been too
much for her to cope with and the director had wanted to make
things easier for her. So in the end, sadly, but not intended, and
without it being anyone's fault, she was the only one in the cast
who had no lines to speak. That obviously hurt her, I think because she had been hoping to make her desire for a child come
true at least in this symbolic form by playing the part of the
mother.

"Gloria swallowed her disappointment and never said a word
about it. She gave a graceful performance; she was praised for it,
and right up to the last, she pretended to be happy with the way
things had gone. But after the performance, some trivial incident
made her suddenly burst into tears. It was right about then that
the woman in charge of her group realized that for some days
Gloria had been listless and unresponsive. She even feared that
Gloria might be going deaf. Gloria kept to herself, went through
another bout of eczema, which everyone thought had been
cured for good, and generally felt as if she'd been put back in the
'waiting room.' In situations like that it all depends on who happens to be with her. If a sensitive caregiver can get her to say
what she has on her mind, the symptoms will disappear quickly.
But sometimes she comes up against someone who preaches
'forgiving and forgetting,' and that only makes everything worse.
What she wants most is to be good, to be the way others want
her to be. But her body puts up a protest. It rebels against that
self-deception. Sometimes it takes months of medical treatment
to get her symptoms back under control.

"When I called Gloria to ask how she was, she said, 'I want to
speak to my child, not just say nothing. It's important for me to
talk to her, the way you've always talked to me.' Fortunately, her
group supervisor had realized what was wrong and helped her

talk about the problem to the director of the play. As before, Gloria's positive physical response to the support she was getting came very quickly."

"In the last few months before she died of cancer," Louise says, "my mother was in a nursing home. The sad thing was that, although some of the nursing staff were very sensitive and sympathetic about the physical symptoms, they paid no attention at all to the emotional causes. My daughter Helen's a social worker, and she says she often gets the impression that genuine, unidealized feelings make some nurses and physicians actively uneasy. Gloria's emotional world is obviously very important to her. All I hope is that she has the same effect on the people looking after her as she did on you. She helped you get back in touch with your own feelings, and now you respect hers. Why shouldn't she succeed with others, too? Maybe she can trigger the same process in some of the people she meets, as she did with you."

"I really hope so," says Nancy earnestly. "It does seem to be the case with some of the staff. But I'm not fooling myself. Gloria is dependent on others and she wants them to like her, so she adjusts to their expectations. She did the same with me, of course, but I'm her mother, and I did what I could to teach her to listen to that voice inside her telling her to say no. She needs someone to help her listen to her own true self because if she doesn't, her body will protest. And if the doctor treating her doesn't understand what it's trying to say, she'll be given unnecessary medication that will only confuse her and make the symptoms even worse. At present, the woman in charge of her group is very good with her, very much attuned to her needs, very sensitive and affectionate. So basically I'm quite optimistic."

"Do you ever find it sad," Louise asks, "that Gloria can't have any part in your intellectual life?"

"Of course I do, but I've had to learn to accept her as she is. Obviously, she has intellectual limitations, but she also has astonishing emotional gifts. What it boils down to is telling myself not to expect the impossible. That hasn't always been easy. I grew up in a family where things of the intellect didn't count for much, and I regretted the absence of any kind of intellectual stimulation. But as a child I didn't get much in the way of affective response, either. And in that area my daughter has enriched my life to no end.

"In a world like ours, where everything is so technical, so faceless, so alienated, people with Down's syndrome can contribute a great deal in terms of human relations. They preserve the enthusiasms and affections a child has and carry them on into adulthood. With her demonstrative, warm-hearted, empathic personality, Gloria has made countless friends for herself. When she was a child, she often used to go and play in a park where old depressed-looking people sat around on benches. Usually we tend to think people like that are best left to themselves and assume they've lost all desire for any kind of contact. But Gloria wasn't bothered by conventions. She would go up to them and say: 'Why are you so sad?' And the faces of those old people lit up with a smile of gratitude. It was then that I realized I didn't need to worry about her future.

"At the same time I've always been fully aware that she cannot take her life into her own hands. She can't handle money or provide for the future, so even as an adult she's bound to remain in a kind of childlike dependency on her mother or on mother substitutes. There are very strict limits to the degree of autonomy people with Down's syndrome can achieve. To organize their lives they need help from persons who are what we call mentally normal. Those persons may not be their equals in terms of emotional development—that was definitely the case with me, for example—which often means that having someone so dependent on them and so different from them is simply too big a challenge. It helps that Gloria's very good at sensing inconsistencies and contradictions in other people's behavior, and if she's given the right kind of support, she can deal with that okay. In the drama group incident, she was finally given the assistance she needed, but it hasn't always been that way."

"How was the birth itself?" Louise asks.

"Easy. And breast-feeding was no problem either, despite our being separated at first. Perhaps you think I can be so relaxed with my daughter because she's not as critical toward me as a mentally normal person would be. But in her own way, she is critical, and her criticisms are very accurate, very matter of fact. She doesn't hold back if she feels I've made a mistake or I've misunderstood her. And I'm very glad she doesn't. It helps us establish a real rapport and clear up any misunderstandings. That's why our relationship is so open; it has scope to develop.

"As a child, Gloria was so completely natural and frank about the help she needed that I had no difficulty in responding in the same way. And she's still as sincere and direct as she ever was. Let me give you an example. She's just turned forty. We spent our last vacation in France, and we went to an exhibition of African art, including a number of sculptures representing mothers with their children. At other exhibitions, like the one we went to with late works by Picasso, Gloria can be very animated in her responses. Here she was surprisingly quiet. Back in the car, she said with tears in her eyes: 'I've got a headache. Why don't those mothers look at their children? It's awful!'

"I stopped the car and took her in my arms. The sculptures had reminded her of the hospital she spent two weeks in just after she was born. 'Why didn't you come?' she asked. 'I belong to you. The people there were just like those women in the exhibition. They changed my diapers and carried me around, but they never looked at me.' A few moments later, she said quite calmly: 'The headache's gone.'

"On the way home I stopped at a store to pick up a book. There were countless magazines lying around, which I scarcely looked at. Suddenly, quite contrary to her normal custom, Gloria grabbed for a magazine called *Terre sauvage*. 'Look!' she said, pointing at the cover, 'that's how you hold a baby.' On the front cover there was a picture of two animals, rodents of some kind, standing on their hind legs, holding on to each other and exchanging an affectionate look. Underneath, it said in French: 'I love, therefore I am.'

"I bought the magazine and read the cover story. It turned out that although the animals on the cover were a little-known species, they'd been around for a million years. They lived in the Kalahari Desert and were particularly affectionate to each other. They're only about ten inches high, and in French they're called *meerkats*. They've even developed a system of baby-sitting. A full-grown animal looks after the babies when their mother's out foraging for food.

"Without my daughter's quick eye, I would hardly have noticed that magazine, and I would never have heard of those creatures and their fascinating habits. I was too busy shielding myself from the overabundance of stimuli all around me. But Gloria has an eye for the essentials. For her, love and affection are always the number-one priority. All the things so many other people strive for—prestige, power, wealth—are unimportant to her, or at least very secondary."

"I can feel how you've benefited deep down. But haven't there been times when it was all too much?"

"Yes, of course there have. Let me tell you a story that'll show you what a mess you can get into. After Richard's death, my inexperience in money matters made me easy prey for speculators. I was worried about Gloria's future, and that made me particularly gullible. When a teacher of disabled children promised me that after my death she would take Gloria in to live with her and look after her, I believed her implicitly and paid her a substantial amount of money in advance. It was only some time later that I realized how cunningly I'd been duped."

"You believed her just like that?" Louise asks in amazement. "Why did you pay her in advance? And no contract or anything?"

"What use would contracts be when I was dead? Contracts obligating someone to take my daughter in and look after her? I was completely convinced of the honesty and sincerity of that woman. At the time, I didn't see what proofs of her good intentions I could have demanded. What mother doesn't want to be sure that her child is provided for? I woke out of my wishful thinking only when I got incontrovertible proof the woman and her boyfriend were frauds. Consequently, she refused to pay back the money she had swindled me out of. Then, of course, I was livid that a professional caretaker should use my disabled daughter to extort money from me to finance the building of a new house Gloria was supposed to move into later."

"She wasn't using your daughter," Louise objects, "she was taking advantage of your situation."

"Right. Anyway, over the years she got me believing in her so completely that I had absolutely no idea what was going on, although as a sociologist I thought I knew all there was to know about manipulation. Today, when I read articles saying that even influential people with a whole team of advisers find it difficult to spot fraud and put the finger on people who've been cheating them, that helps me to be a bit less hard on myself for being such a fish. I had no advisers, only my troubles and my concern for Gloria's future well-being.

"Having been through all that, I now know that it's easy to fall victim to manipulation if you've taken on more responsibility than you can handle. I wanted to make sure my daughter would be all right after my death. That was simply too much for me to handle. It's an experience that's taught me not to feel so responsible for others, not even for my daughter.

"I've already given her all I can give her. For someone with her disability, she's relatively self-assured, she's incredibly good-natured, she's outgoing and friendly, and I'm sure she'll meet plenty of people who will be protective to her instead of taking advantage of her. When something upsets her, she can't always say what it is, and that makes her dependent on whoever's looking after her, but basically it's in her nature to be happy. You just have to let her be."

Louise is appalled. "But that's incredible! A woman calling herself a trained caregiver and exploiting your worries about Gloria's future to build herself a new house. How did you discover it was a swindle? Or did it all come out on its own?"

"It certainly wasn't easy. It was a complicated, upsetting business, first vague suspicions, then greater certainty, right up to the final climax. And not only because both of them were so good at putting up a front. The thing was that for a long time I didn't want to believe that the results of my inquiries really were the truth. Maybe I'll tell you the whole thing sometime. Right now, I'd prefer not to think about it. It was such a horrible mess I don't want to spoil your visit by talking about it."

"Maybe in your position I'd have let myself be fooled, too. But when there's an important decision to make, I can always consult with my family. One of my sons-in-law is a lawyer; my husband's an experienced businessman. I'm never alone with things like that. Also, I think women in my kind of position don't get approached with such propositions. Professional swindlers choose their victims very carefully. A widow in late middle age with a disabled child—you were the ideal target."

"Maybe I was conditioned to be easy game right from the outset. Predators sense that immediately. As a child, I learned very early to close my eyes to unpleasant facts and pin my hopes to empty promises. I wanted to believe my parents loved me as they said they did, even though the way they treated me told a completely different story. And when someone came along and said they really liked Gloria and she should come and live with them, I wanted to believe that, as well. I wanted it so badly that I was willing to give all the money I had been left by my parents to make it come true.

"I thought it made good sense to invest that money in my daughter's future, like a belated gift from her grandparents, who had never taken any interest in her when they were alive. That wishful thinking reinforced my gullibility, and this woman and her boyfriend exploited it to the full. But now I've shaken off that wishful thinking for good. More than ever before I feel confident that my daughter's going to be all right, and I hope and believe that most of the people she meets will be honest and sincere. If that happens, she won't have any need of her grandparents' money."

IN THE plane back to New York, Louise thinks of her daughter Helen and little Sara, the grandchild who made her feel so uneasy. That's all in the past now. For the first time since Sara was born, Louise feels free of the burden of pity.

Maybe, she thinks, maybe Gloria's story will be a lot less surprising for Helen than it was for me. She seems so attached to her daughter, in a way I wouldn't have thought possible before. But now I find it much less of a mystery. As for Nancy, she seems much more open, relaxed, and fulfilled than she was when we were students. And doesn't she have Gloria to thank for that?

MARGOT AND LILKA

Warsaw to Sydney and Back

MARGOT IS too happy for words. This morning a new patient
has come for an appointment, and she recognizes her as an old
school friend from Warsaw.

Margot emigrated from Poland to Australia in 1946, and in all
that time she has been back only once. It was 1950. The huge
posters of Stalin in the streets killed any lingering desire she
might have had to go back for good, but even before that she
knew she could never feel at home again in a country where
she survived the Holocaust only because she had faked documents with which she could pass herself off as Aryan. Much of
what she saw in Poland reminded her of what she had gone
through just to stay alive.

She is sitting in her office with the new patient opposite her,

Mrs. Rogers, an American woman accompanying her husband on a business trip to Australia. She has come to consult Margot about an allergy problem. At first there is nothing to indicate that the two women might know each other; their surnames are different from the ones they had as children, and their faces are sixty years older. But the name "Lilka" awakens in Margot memories of the prewar years in Warsaw and those long conversations in her friend's room in the house on Dluga Street.

Still half lost in the reverie caused by those memories, she says: "I used to know a girl called Lilka, but that was a long time ago, in another world . . ."

Her patient starts scrutinizing the face of the woman sitting opposite her. After a while she says shyly: "You don't happen to come from Warsaw yourself, do you?"

This simple, straightforward question is followed by a long silence. Why doesn't Margot say yes without further ado? Because saying yes or no means making an important decision. Because the question stirs up things Margot has long since buried deep down inside herself. Do I really want to start delving into my past again? she asks herself. It's not easy to explain your own life to others so that they can really understand. And anyway, why should I? I'm not going to delude myself into hoping that someone else might really take an interest in what I went through all those years ago. I know by experience that it's out of the question. But do I really know? How can I know? How can I say that so flatly? Because I haven't had any luck so far? This may be Lilka, the friend of my school days. If anyone can understand me, she will. Why shouldn't I be open with her?

The new patient sits quietly waiting for Margot's answer. She feels a lump in her throat; her eyes are filling with tears. She already senses who Margot is, but she simply cannot grasp it yet.

Margot knows the silence has gone on much too long. But

she needs time. Inside her, there's a long, long bridge to cross, the bridge from her present, ordered existence in Sydney back through the expanses of time to the prewar years in Warsaw. Is that what I want? she asks herself. Do I want to hear Lilka's story? Do I want to tell her mine?

Deep down, she already knows the answer. She wants to talk and she knows instinctively she can cope with this encounter. As soon as she can admit that to herself, she asks hesitatingly: "But you're not Lilka Gold from Dluga Street, are you?" "Yes, I am," says Mrs. Rogers. "And you're Marysia Fenner from Orla Street, aren't you?"

The sound of those names that Margot had to erase from her memory in 1942 is enough to break down the barriers, to dispel the distance between this Australian doctor and her American patient. As they embrace, they both feel suddenly transported back to the time before they were forced to manipulate their memories and submit to the alienation from their own true selves. Margot invites Lilka to come to her house for the evening. And that night the former school friends sit in Margot's living room and talk almost without stopping until well into the small hours. They both have so much to tell, but they are equally eager to hear what the other has been through. And for Margot that feeling of passionate mutual interest and concern is like a wonderful, unexpected gift.

After emigrating in 1946, she quickly got used to the idea that no one was interested in the stories of people from Poland. There was much talk of the camps, of course, but the extent of the suffering they stood for was so great that it was beyond people's capacity to take it in. Margot herself felt that compared to the prisoners in the concentration camps she had had a relatively easy time of it. So she quickly trained herself not to say anything about her past. Instead she learned to listen to others.

Her husband, an Australian, is kind enough but not much of a listener. He has no inclination to be reminded about the war in Europe. In the course of time, all this made Margot's silence more and more profound. But then she started longing to find someone who would enable her to break that silence, someone who could bear to hear what she had to tell, perhaps because they had been through something similar themselves. And now, all of a sudden, without any effort or any searching on her part, her wish has come true.

It begins harmlessly enough: "Remember how we fooled the geography teacher and played hooky to go wandering around town? And that wonderful smell coming from the cake shop on Nowy Swiat? Whenever I think of the main street, I smell those doughnuts. And do you ever think back to those times we used to go sneaking down to Panska Street to watch the prostitutes? Heavens, how curious we were, how intrigued, and how scared!"

But then, abruptly, one of them asks the inevitable question that takes them back to that other world, a world of fear, a world in which millions suffered inexpressible horrors: "Where were you when the war broke out?" Margot asks. And Lilka starts to tell her story.

"At the outbreak of war, in 1939, I was in Radomsko, living in a tenement block belonging to my paternal grandparents. There was a big orchard behind the house, and I spent a lot of time there on my own, reading under the trees or doing my homework in the shed. On the day war was declared, September 1, 1939, we dug a big trench in the orchard and spent the whole of the first day in it, hoping it would protect the family from the shrapnel. But the next day already the refugees started passing through on their long trek from the western border, and we followed their example. We snatched up everything we could lay our hands on and fled out into the country, thinking that way we'd be safe from the Germans, from the bombs. Actually we had no very clear idea about what it was exactly that we were fleeing from.

"It was a headlong, mindless mass exodus; the panic was in-credible. My youngest aunt on my father's side knew some well-to-do people, and they took her and her husband and daughter with them to the eastern border in their car. The only chance we had was to join the procession of refugees heading for Warsaw on foot and taking as many of their belongings with them as they could carry—pictures of saints, eiderdowns, saucepans, and anything else that seemed important to them. On the way we frequently had to throw ourselves flat on the ground because the German fighter pilots were flying low and shooting at civilians. That made the panic and the chaos even worse. Most people soon realized it was pointless trying to escape. They turned back that same day and waited in their own homes for the German troops to arrive. But not us. We didn't stop to think. We managed to get friends of ours to take our grandparents with them, while we kept on heading for Warsaw, mostly on foot. Sometimes we got a ride on a farmcart or took a local train, but most of the time we walked.

"Our overriding concern was not to fall into the clutches of the invaders. But ultimately, the course we opted for was worse than the German occupation, at least in the first few months. Of course, we didn't know that then. We thought Warsaw was bound to put up some kind of resistance.

"I still have a very clear memory of all those nights we spent out in the open. Every time dawn broke, the rising sun filled me with the irrational hope that we might be spared after all. We slept on the ground, usually for short periods only, since time was pressing. Every day, the stream of refugees grew bigger. A week later, we finally reached Warsaw and were taken in by my aunts, who lived on Orla Street. At almost exactly the same time, the German armies arrived outside the city and a four-week siege began. It was a terrible time. The bombardments went on almost without interruption. We hardly had anything to eat and spent most of the time in the bomb shelters. I'm sure you know what that was like; you were in Warsaw yourself at the time.

"When the Germans had finally taken Warsaw, we went back to Radomsko in an oxcart. Here, the first few weeks of the war had been relatively uneventful—no bombs, no shortage of food. The horrors we'd been through had all been in vain. I don't know what made us do it; perhaps it was because my mother was so afraid, perhaps because I wanted to see my aunts in Warsaw. I was very fond of them. My father didn't seem to care much, one way or the other."

"I don't really remember your father very well," Margot says. "I knew your mother and you always told me a lot about her. All I know about your father is that you were very fond of him. But I can't really picture him at the moment." ·

"That's just the thing, Margot! Fifty years after he died I still loved him, but I never really knew what he was like. I idealized him as a victim of the Holocaust and never dared to admit to myself how he confused me as a child by not being frank with me. And the story of my first love is a precise reflection of what I went through with my father."

"Do you want to tell me about it? You first left Warsaw in 1938, so you must have been fourteen at the time. After that I never heard from you again."

"I spent the last summer before the war with a cousin who lived in the country," Lilka says. "The evening before I left, I met a fifteen-year-old boy, Janek, and fell in love with him. I can still see him now: tall, black-haired, gray eyes, a warm, cheerful, almost laughing voice. We went on a long walk through the fields, and he put his arm around my shoulders and talked a lot about himself. I can't remember what. There were no declarations, no protestations, just a feeling of happiness that I've never forgotten. He lived in Poznan, and we wrote to each other, very prim, lofty letters about literature and politics. It sounds odd, I know, considering how old we were. But I was obviously using my intellect to shield off the strong feelings I didn't dare express, not least because I was suspicious of them. I had no experience in handling my feelings. And yet I was so head over heels in love I couldn't think of anything else.

"One day, our teacher announced that the class would be going on a trip to Poznan. I was walking on air. I still remember talking to my father about it, trying to tell him I was in love and needed five zloty for the trip. That's the only conversation with my father I can remember. For a long time I believed it was a good conversation, that he had shown real fatherly concern. It was only much later that I realized the harm he did to me with what he said. He gave me the money, and I went on the trip. But he told me I mustn't have any illusions. Love and real life were two different things. Loving someone was no reason for getting married. That message must have made a strong impression on me, although it was only my father's own personal experience that made him say it: his parents had forbidden him to marry the girl he loved. Anyway, that view of his took root deep inside me. And I married my first husband, although I didn't love him. It was as if I was unconsciously trying to confirm my father's philosophy.

"Janek came to Radomsko in 1940 and stayed there till 1942. He wrote me countless letters, insisting that he loved me, but it was all very literary and intellectual. In all that time there was nothing physical between us. I assumed that, intellectual as he was, he wasn't interested in that kind of intimacy. But it wasn't true at all. Much later he told me he'd been having sexual relations with other women at the same time as he was sending me his love poems. But he never showed me any physical affection. I don't know why he kept his sensuality and his desires from me, and I don't know what it was about me that made him do so. He never told me.

"I was longing to be close to someone, physically close. That was what drove me into the arms of another man, a teacher much older than I was, a man I admired and who appeared to respond to my longing for tenderness and spiritual intercourse. But soon I was forced to realize that I had been a victim of my imagination and my illusions. In fact, he was never open and frank with me. Unlike Janek, he wasn't a Jew, but the Gestapo were after him because he was in the Polish resistance movement. He escaped to Warsaw before the deportations started. Later he helped me to find a room there, and that was really a lot in those days."

"How did you get to Warsaw?"

"I asked my school friend Wanda for help; she was a Catholic, and she was kind and brave enough to lend me her identity card for a few days. I didn't say anything to my parents; they would only have tried to stop me. They didn't believe that the danger threatening us was as inescapable. I did. I went to Warsaw with Wanda's passport in my pocket. And on the way from the station to my lodgings I saw Jewish families being herded along the streets with small bundles in their arms. My heart heaved with indignation, but I couldn't show it. I pretended that those poor hunted creatures were no concern of mine, and I imitated all those other Poles whose blank faces showed no sign of protest or dismay.

"As you know, all that barbarity in full view of everyone on the streets was tolerated in silence by most of the Polish population, as if it was something quite normal. So I learned to bite back my feelings as well. That afternoon I banished them from my heart for a long time to come. I went to the landlady, where my teacher friend had rented rooms for me, and told her I had grown up with my parents in the provinces and had come to Warsaw to study. The woman was kind and friendly and believed me, with no question asked. And in a way it was true—up to a point. Later, when I was in touch with the underground and the secret university, I was able to get myself an identity card of my own. I sent Wanda her passport and that was that. I had fake documents made for other people as well, for Janek, my sister, my parents, my uncle, and one of my aunts. Janek still goes by the surname I thought up for him then. It's the only link we have left."

"Did you live together in Warsaw?"

"In Warsaw I hardly saw Janek at all. It was a case of every man for himself. We met only a couple of times and talked about the horrors we knew were in store for us. In 1944, during the Polish uprising, I ran into him once again. He was a sergeant in the rebel Polish army, stationed near the place where I lived. It was the first time we spent the night together, the first and only time we lived out our love for each other. In the midst of all that chaos, the chance encounter was like a miracle, an overwhelming piece of luck, a happy chance that seemed to augur well for the future. It was like a return to my own self, to my first love, a love that I had been unfaithful to by embarking on that brief relationship with the teacher. Like everybody else, we were euphoric at the success of the first military liberation coup. But it didn't last. The very next day Janek and his platoon had to go out again to fight. And that same day my sister and I were buried up to our necks in rubble in the cellar of the house next door after a bomb attack. We both looked as if someone had dropped us in a bowl of flour, but at least we weren't badly injured.

"That was in August 1944. I lost all contact with Janek, but the hope of seeing him again kept me alive and active. No sooner was there any movement on the front lines than I hopped onto a truck and went in search of him. That was in January 1945. There were indications that he must have holed up in the Polish mountains. I hitched another ride, and a few days later I arrived there completely exhausted, with big holes in my shoes. It was cold; there was snow everywhere. I had no idea at the time that a girl traveling alone in that region was likely to get raped. But nothing happened to me. The Russian drivers were friendly and quite willing to give me a ride.

"No, the worst thing was meeting Janek. He was so remote, so distant. I didn't know the reason, but he seemed all hard and cold and different inside. All my longings suddenly seemed completely inappropriate. Much later I learned that he had a new girl friend. But he didn't say anything at the time. We even resolved to live together in Poznan. My mind was unwilling to admit that there was something wrong, but my body reacted immediately. It was on the way to Poznan, on the back of a cattle car, that I felt the first painful symptoms of some illness. My body knew that I was lying to myself; it was my mind that refused to register the fact. Janek and I moved in together for a few weeks, until I was finally committed to the hospital.

"On May 8, with the bells ringing to greet the end of the war, I was lying in a hospital bed with raging fever and severe polyarthritis. Despite the pains in my joints, I was happy. The organized manhunt was at an end. Today I believe that my illness was the manifestation of all the emotional pains I had bitten back during the wartime years and also the expression of the truth about my personal situation, a truth that I had done my best to deny. Nobody saw it that way at the time, least of all me. So I let them take my tonsils out and a few completely sound teeth because the tonsils were diagnosed as being responsible for the infection. But the symptoms refused to go away.

"It was only when my mother visited me in the hospital and told me the truth about Janek that the pains started receding. She said that Janek was getting married to a woman I didn't even know existed. It hurt. But the effects of the truth were spectacular. It was as if a blanket of mist had started rising, as if I had finally been given fresh air to breathe, to help me recover. As long as I had deceived myself and ignored the signs, I had been doing violence to my body.

"About thirty years after the war, I met Janek again in New York. His first wife had died of cancer, and his second wife had the same illness. Only now, as an adult, did I realize that he'd always been inclined to dissemble. That meeting told me that we could never have had an open, honest relationship. And love without openness is something I cannot imagine. For what is love but the willingness to open your heart, to show yourself as you are, and to accept, understand, and like the other person as he is, instead of trying to change him?

"My infatuation was a thing of the past; it was a part of my youth, part of a time in my life in which my suspicion of my own feelings and overreliance on my intellect had determined my choices. In the course of time, I also realized that much of my partiality for Janek had to do with the sound of his voice. When we were forced to keep in touch by letter, when all I had were the written words on the page, my judgments about him were much more down to earth.

"Janek was almost always kind, charming, and helpful. He was greatly concerned to live up to other people's expectations. He wanted to be liked and admired, and usually he succeeded.

But his all-consuming desire for intellectual and moral recognition left little room for any kind of emotional life. In those few days in New York, I also realized that we had never really been as closely attuned intellectually as I had always believed."

"It sounds as if after all those years living under an assumed identity it was actually yourself you were looking for when you went on that desperate search for Janek. You keep saying that you were lying to yourself. But how could you have found out the truth if he was keeping it from you? I mean, you'd never have gone to Poznan in a cattle car to start a new life with him if you'd known he was going to get married to someone else. Why don't you say that you'd been deceived?"

"It wasn't so easy for me to do that as you think. I told myself that he didn't intend to lie to me; he just didn't have the courage to tell me the truth. And that was something I knew only too well from my father. I have no idea why Janek didn't have the courage. I can only guess, since he never told me much about his family. In fact, I hardly knew him at all."

"You're saying you loved a man you didn't know?"

"Yes. I loved a man who never showed me his true self, a man who was so preoccupied with himself that he never really knew I was there. A replica of my childhood. In our relationship with each other, we both loved a phantom, although I was besotted with that phantom much longer than he was. Probably because my relationship with my father had been based on illusions as well. I wanted him to love me, so I believed in them. I refused to face up to the fact that my father was always evading me, that he was never there when I needed him, that he never protected me, and that in the last resort he didn't really care what became of me. If I had realized that in my youth, I would have been more wary of Janek, particularly as my own body gave me plenty of warnings. It's not Janek's fault that I learned to deceive myself when I was a child. For a long time my memories of Janek were important to me because they stood for the unspoiled world I lived in before the war and the experiences we shared during the war.

"There was one event during the ghetto years in Radomsko that really forged a bond between us. The inhabitants were forbidden to leave the town under threat of death. But one magnificent summer's day in 1942 we simply flouted that ban and went for a long walk in the countryside, down by the Warta River. The gardens lining the path were full of flowers, zinnias and mallows. Everything was quiet and peaceful, as if life was still the same as it had always been. In fact, the end was near. We knew all about the deportations. That outing meant an enormous amount to me and helped me to sustain the hope that I would not just somehow survive but that I might look forward to a life of happiness.

"That hope kept me alive. So I clung to it even though I sensed that it was an illusion. I couldn't afford to abandon my illusions, not yet. So I fell ill. It wasn't until thirty years later that I had the fortitude, the experience to see things realistically. As a twenty-one-year-old girl, exhausted by war, I was still the child who wanted to understand everyone else but who ignored her own distress. So that distress had to express itself as physical pain; it had no other outlet."

"You say you would have been quicker accepting the truth about Janek if you hadn't learned to live with the fact that your father was always evading you when you were a child. What exactly did he do?"

"As I said, I don't have many memories of him. But looking back, I have the feeling my father always kept out of my way, as if he had something to hide, like Janek. If it hadn't been for the war, the struggle to survive, I might have been quicker to discover my father's real character. I might have found someone to talk to about it, and that would have stopped me making lots of wrong decisions in later life. Ultimately, the affair with Janek was just one of a whole string of vain attempts to evade the truth and preserve the illusion of being loved."

"And how were things for you after the war, in America?"

"An uncle of mine in Boston got me a visa. So I went to Boston and studied psychology. Suddenly I found myself in a country of miracles. If I had ever had roots anywhere else, it could have been a paradise for me. But all I brought with me to America was loneliness and isolation. Everyone was kind to me but I felt like a stranger who had landed there by chance. I felt that no one could have the remotest idea what we had been through in Poland, and deep down nobody really wanted to know. And that way I ended up marrying Viktor, a Polish student who had come to Boston on a study grant and decided to stay there. We didn't really have much in common, but in that foreign country he as a Pole at least had some inkling of what it meant to have been a Jew in Poland during the war. And that was important for me. He himself wasn't Jewish, but he had been there when the Germans came, and he knew all about the things that had happened to me."

"I can certainly understand that," says Margot. "He was at least someone who had witnessed what had been going on, and you obviously needed that desperately. And you could speak Polish together."

"Well, at the beginning we did," says Lilka, rather sadly. "Later we spoke English so that our daughter could understand us. Unfortunately, we never taught her Polish properly. Viktor and I agreed in many of our judgments about American society, and I was able to talk to him about my dislike of the Communist regime in Poland because I knew he was of the same opinion.

All these shared opinions blinded me to the huge differences in our characters. I had no idea who I was or what my needs were; I didn't know that it's possible to have a relationship that doesn't cost a tremendous effort to keep going. All those attempts to forget my own identity during the war had sort of put my feelings in cold storage. The disappointment with Janek made it worse because I didn't allow myself to feel it to the full. It was as if I were turned to stone, paralyzed."

"Do you think," Margot asks, "that it was that kind of emotional numbness that stopped you from realizing that the marriage wasn't working out for either of you?"

"Yes, but it wasn't the only reason, Margot. The whole thing was a rerun of what I had been through with Janek. I went on fooling myself because I didn't want to give up my desire for a meaningful relationship. At the time I just wasn't able to sustain that kind of relationship with all that buried history inside me, but the desire for it was so strong that I kept on trying. I went to a psychoanalyst and for a time I felt a little closer to Viktor, more open toward him, but it didn't last. A few weeks later we were back to square one. The torments of speechlessness. Finally, we got a divorce. Much later I remarried, a Jew this time, and we've been together now for several years. There've been conflicts between us, too, but we can always talk them over. I find life easier now, much easier than it used to be. Looking back, I just can't believe that I was willing to live in that kind of alienation for so long. Well, I've told you about me. What was it like for you between 1940 and 1945? You were in Warsaw, too."

"Yes, first in the ghetto, with my parents. Then my father got me a false identity card with the help of a business partner of his. He saved my life. Shortly afterward, he was deported. . . . My mother stayed in the ghetto, where she was allowed to work in a factory for a while. Then I got her out, together with my sister.

Looking back, it was like one long battle with an endless succession of extortionists. Like you, I had no trouble finding a room because my identity card looked so genuine. As soon as I had a fairly secure base to work from, I started looking for a convent school in the country that I could send my sister to. Finally, I succeeded. The nuns guessed the truth about her identity on the very first day, but they took her in and cared for her lovingly all the same. My sister was baptized there. It was an incredible piece of luck being able to get her in there without any of the usual connections. The only reason it worked out at all was that it was the early days yet, 1942, before the ghettos were dissolved. After that, thousands of Jews started looking for refuge under false names. And as you know, that meant either being very rich or having very good connections."

"Where did you find the strength to save your mother and sister?"

"In those years in Warsaw I was entirely dependent on my intuition. I was acting on hunches, living on my nerves. I had to be creative if I was going to survive. Maybe that was what gave me the self-confidence and the strength I needed. Every new situation was a challenge. There was no previous experience to go on. I taught German in the underground secondary school; that way I earned just enough to keep my head above water. But as you know, for a Jew with false papers, staying alive took more than the money for the rent and three meals a day. You had to be on your guard all the time, like hunted game. Worst was having to worry about being denounced by people you knew.

"The extortionists were no fools. After my father was deported, my mother took an assumed name and went into hiding with the false documents I obtained for her. But I couldn't take her in to live with me. The atmosphere in Warsaw was already poisoned by suspicion and denunciations. My mother looked

Jewish, and at the very sight of her my landlady would have
guessed the truth about me straightaway. So I answered a small
'room to let' ad in the paper, made an appointment, and went
there along with my mother. What I didn't know was that the
prospective landlady was an extortionist herself. She operated
undercover using accomplices to do the dirty work. They followed us up the stairs when we arrived, accosted us, passed
themselves off as Polish police detectives, and threatened to hand
us over to the Gestapo. They would have pocketed a reward for
turning us in. The whole thing was a bluff, of course, but the way
things were, there was a good chance of them getting lucky. I expect they tried the same trick on dozens of other potential
lodgers, and most of the time they probably got what they
wanted. They weren't risking anything because Jews had no legal
rights.

"At the last moment I realized it was money they were after.
I had no money myself; all I possessed was a ring. I offered it to
them. Unfortunately, I had left the ring at home. They went
there with us, and from then on they knew where I lived. I had
to explain to my landlady why I had suddenly turned up with
my 'aunt' and these strange men. A few days later, some other
men appeared. They had probably been given the address by the
first group of extortionists. On their arrival, they chanced on a
sixteen-year-old girl that my landlady had been hiding in a room
in the house for a considerable sum of money. I had never noticed she was there.

"The men said they were from the Gestapo, and I was convinced this was finally the end of the line. I had no more jewelry,
so the girl and I had no choice but to go with them to the
Gestapo headquarters. At the last moment it suddenly occurred
to me to ask the girl whether she had any money with her. She
said she did and naively asked whether that would do her any

good. We helped each other. I told her what to do, and she bailed us both out. So we both escaped by the skin of our teeth. But now I had to look for somewhere else to live. I had already made temporary arrangements for my mother.

"I lived with this constant strain for three years. My sister had left the convent school some time before. She had been committed to a Warsaw hospital for treatment of a violent attack of shingles. After the Polish uprising broke out in 1944, I took her in with me. My sister and I escaped by crossing the Vistula River by night. The other side of the river was liberated territory.

"I know of nobody else who got away by crossing the Vistula. Perhaps it was a unique opportunity, limited to that one particular night. I asked various survivors of the uprising, but none of them had heard of civilians getting away that way. But in a book[1] someone sent me from Germany recently, there's a passage that does refer to this escape route. It was written by a Jewish woman who also survived by pretending to be Aryan. A friend of hers reports that many people tried to get away by crossing the Vistula, but the boats were shot at and sank. She herself was wounded on the riverbank and lost consciousness.

"For a long time I lived in hope that perhaps there may have been others lucky enough to cross to safety. But I've never come across any. I would have given anything to talk to someone about the escape, someone who'd been through it, too. Perhaps not everyone was in such a hurry to escape that way. At the time it was generally assumed that in a few days the front would have moved. People thought the end of the Nazis was in sight, and it was another repeat performance of the old Polish uprisings with their lack of political strategic realism. Countless governments have exploited the courage of the Polish people, their readiness to stand up for human liberty and dignity, and never shown the slightest political perspicacity themselves. Of course, when we two were still singing along with those patriotic anthems at school, I didn't think that way. But even during the uprising, I found it impossible to identify with that tub-thumping romantic jingoism. When the uprising was quelled, were you taken to that camp in Pruszkow like everyone else?"

"Yes, but go on with your story. I want to hear how you got across the Vistula."

"There were Polish soldiers in the Soviet army, and they put across to our side of the river in small boats to build a bridge-head. They were picking up the wounded and taking them back across the river in the boats. We asked them if we could go along, too. The soldiers said it was risky because the Germans were sending up flares over the river and shooting at everything that moved. They said it was up to us to decide. We just couldn't face the idea of submitting to the Nazis after nine weeks of free-dom. I'd risk anything rather than do that. My sister didn't ob-ject; she left it to me to decide. So we got into one of the boats and crossed the river unharmed, despite all the flares. And a few moments later we were racing up the riverbank, across ground that was burning beneath our feet, through an area that had been under constant bombardment. We ran as fast as we could, think-ing that someone was after us. Finally, we found refuge for the rest of the night in the courtyard of an abandoned house. It wasn't till next morning that we noticed that our faces were black with soot and smoke. We set off again and arrived at a vil-lage. The people were as scared of us as if we'd been sent by the devil himself with news that something horrible was about to happen.

"The villagers had no idea what was going on across the river, so it was hard to explain what had happened to us. But in the end one woman took us into her house for us to wash our faces. After that we could resume our journey. Finally, we arrived at a medical outpost where I was given work looking after soldiers with stomach wounds that were festering. I can still remember the smell. But by then I was so groggy even that couldn't knock me over. Hope that the war would soon be over kept me going.

"For a long time I had no inclination to go back to Poland. Sometimes I feel a kind of nostalgia for the countryside there, the quiet rivers, the cornfields, the mallows in the farmhouse gardens. For years I planted mallows in my own garden, probably to keep my happy childhood memories. I'd like to meet and talk to my former friends in Warsaw, but now things there will have changed out of all recognition. My mother died a long time ago. And I've lost all contact with my sister."

Lilka has the same feeling of ambivalence: longing for the landscapes of her childhood, fear of the memories of her youth. Neither of them wants to dwell on this subject any longer. Finally, Margot breaks the silence.

"We obviously had similar experiences back then, but my life has been less problematic than yours, Lilka. Of course, I've often felt lonely here in Australia with no one to talk to about what I went through in Poland. But I've still managed to put down roots. There's my husband first of all, his kindness and sincerity. Then I was lucky enough to study medicine and met interesting people who soon became friends. I get on very well with my children. You could have had all that in America, too. But you sound as if you've had one long series of bad breaks."

"You're right," says Lilka. "Although we had much the same time of it in the war, our lives have taken completely different courses. But we also grew up very differently, you and I. I well remember the atmosphere at your house. Your mother was a very warmhearted person, and I sensed that she loved you and was always encouraging toward you. That was a feeling I never had with my mother. I always felt as if I was on trial, and later my first husband was a man who made me feel exactly the same. Your father got you an identity card, and that was your passport to life and freedom. The way he made sure you got your documents shows how much foresight he had. Many Jewish parents reacted that way when the deportations started. They entrusted their small children to Christian families. But you weren't a baby anymore; you were nineteen. And yet your father looked after you first.

"With me, it was the other way around. My father was like a child. He refused to see the danger and took no responsibility either for himself or anyone else. When I decided to leave the Radomsko ghetto and escape to Warsaw, I was nineteen, too, but I had to hide my plan from my parents. They would have stopped me from going. Once I had gone, my father supposedly said that I must have been in a really big hurry to get away from him, and he just felt abandoned. And that's the difference between us."

"I once went to Israel," Margot says. "In search of my roots, I suppose. I didn't find them, though. My daughter's boyfriend is an Israeli; they're getting married soon. That'll be a kind of unexpected return to things Jewish for me. I imagine you've been to Israel yourself. How did you feel there?"

"I was there last in 1978. I remember crying in the taxi on the way back to the airport. What I wanted most in the world was to stay in Jerusalem. I loved that city. There were so many people there who had memories just like mine. But Jewish orthodoxy is something I can't stomach at any price. So I doubt that I could have lived in Israel and still felt I was really free.

"If I had emigrated to Israel, my life would certainly have been different, but I don't think it would have been any easier. I imagine I could have got on reasonably good terms with a number of people. I could have shared my memories with them; our destinies would have given us something in common. And the Jewish music you hear all over the place there would have done me good, too. Even today, I still respond very emotionally to the rhythms and melodies of Jewish songs, the sadness in them, the humor, the specific Yiddish accent I heard in my grandparents' house as a child, though I understood only half of what they said—my parents spoke Polish to us children. That was what made the Yiddish songs so fascinating.

"On the other hand, I felt like a stranger when I visited the orthodox quarter in Jerusalem in the seventies. I had no such feelings in the Museum of Jerusalem or in the kibbutz I went to, only in that orthodox part of the city. I had come in search of memories, a world I was familiar with, but I felt as if I had landed in Kafka's *Castle*. But perhaps I did find my own brand of truth there, in that feeling of total isolation among people who didn't seem to notice I was there. It was as if I were made of glass. It was exactly the way I felt in my grandparents' house as a child.

"Somehow my memories of Jewish rites and customs are bound up with the impression that they're more about constraints and duties, tradition and obedience than about communication and love. I expect that feeling has its roots in the way nothing ever got talked about at home. In that respect I'll always remember the Seder service we had when I was seven. There I stood, ready to ask the Hebrew questions I had learned by heart. I was full of pleasurable anticipation, thinking that someone would respond to these questions and give me an answer at last.

"The first question was: What is the difference between this night and all other nights? Why do we eat both kinds of bread all the year, but today only matzo? For me, personally, that meant: Father, why are you prepared to listen to me and answer my questions today. What makes today so different? But it wasn't any different. Once the questions were asked, that was the end of it for me. Nobody so much as dreamed that the child might be expecting an intelligible explanation. The right and wise answers to the questions were all set down in the Haggadah. In the traditional way, this was read out loud by the adults in Hebrew, and it took several hours. Although I didn't understand a word, I had to sit there quietly and listen.

"Today, that first memory of the Seder has a highly symbolic significance for me. It was there that I first sensed how pointless it was trying to engage in any kind of communication with my parents. I see myself, my disappointment at being left alone with my questions. Actually they were answering my questions, in detail, for a matter of hours but in a language I didn't understand. They acted that way because they had been taught to do so by their parents. The Exodus had always been celebrated as if it had happened yesterday. I spent all my life trying to get my father to talk to me, but it never happened. That loneliness in the house of my parents, and the expression it took in that first Seder service, is why on big social occasions I've never really felt like I 'belong.'

"It wasn't until after my divorce that I got back in touch with my submerged Jewish identity. That same year I traveled to Jerusalem, I discovered the city and the whole country, Yam Kinneret, the desert, Masada, and the works of Martin Buber. Just like when I was young, I was seduced into loving the place and hoping to find my spiritual home there. I say 'seduced' because I didn't find that home there; rather, I found it in myself, in my feelings during my stay there. Then, after returning to America, I met my present husband. He grew up in a Jewish family in Boston, studied there, and is just as critical of orthodoxy as I am. His family is very liberal, open-minded, and I feel at ease with them.

"Hearing Yiddish and Hebrew spoken, hearing the songs they sing in Israel were the things that revived those withered feelings of my youth, put me back in touch with my old identity, and helped me to build a new one on top of it. I could never have done that in my first marriage. It wasn't Viktor's fault or anyone else's. I needed all those years to come to terms with the horrors of the war. And to do that, I first had to admit to myself that they were horrors, even though I was never confined in a concentration camp. There's no common denominator to describe that process, and I'm not going to try. I want to leave all those different feelings as they are and see how they develop."

"Strange," says Margot. "Listening to you talking about Jewishness awakened memories in me that I thought I had left behind in 1942. Suddenly, I see my Uncle Aaron's house—he was my mother's brother. His wife, my Aunt Dora, came from a religious family and was very keen on observing the old Jewish customs. She loved her father very much, and he had the reputation of being very kind and good-natured. In her new home she wanted to celebrate the Jewish festivities in the same way as her parents had done. They lived some distance from Warsaw, in Otwock, and sometimes they invited me to go and stay with them for a few days. It was there that I made the acquaintance of the Jewish traditions that my parents no longer cultivated. I remember Uncle Aaron telling us about the meaning of Hannukah, and my two cousins and I listened with rapt attention. He read us stories by Jewish authors, in Polish translation so that we could understand them. Without those experiences, I would hardly have any way of relating to what you've just been talking about. In 1942 I locked that world away and really and truly forgot all about it. Not even talking to my future son-in-law, a real live, flesh-and-blood Israeli, did anything help me regain access to all that. He belongs to a different generation and has very little knowledge of the world of the Polish Jews. But you come from that world, and like me you've been 'unfaithful' to it. I can finally talk to you. I'd even like to go back to Poland once if you'd come with me. With you I'd have the courage. Because we could talk about our impressions. That might help me to bear the unbearable, to withstand the pain. What do you say, Lilka?"

Lilka is silent for a while. She feels hesitant. "I don't know. I wanted never to go back. Since I got divorced, I've hardly spoken any Polish, only here with you. But one thing's for sure. If I do decide to go, it'll be with you. Let's give it a little time. After all, we'll be staying in touch."

REFLECTIONS

GURUS AND CULT LEADERS

How They Function

MANY PROBLEMS APPEAR in a new light when we look to childhood as a source of possible explanations. We are living in an age in which democracies are gaining the upper hand over dictatorships. At the same time the cult-group phenomenon is an indication that there is a growth in the number of totalitarian systems to which people voluntarily submit themselves. People growing up in a spirit of liberty and tolerance, accepted in childhood for what they are, rather than being throttled and stunted by their upbringing, would hardly place themselves at the mercy of a cult group of their own accord. And if by chance or skillful manipulation, they did fall afoul of such an organization, they certainly would not stay there very long.

But many people joining such groups seem completely

indifferent to the fact that their new surroundings are powered by mechanisms expressly designed to subjugate them, to rob them of the freedom to think, to act, and to feel as they see fit. They seem completely impervious to the fact that such groups set out to impose an Orwellian form of surveillance and a demand for mindless obedience from which the prospects of escaping are more or less nil. Years of brainwashing and indoctrination ensure that the victims are kept unaware of the insidious harm being done to their personalities. They have no notion of the price they have paid for their malleability because they have no notion that there is any alternative.

The thing that concerns me most about cult groups is the unconscious manipulation that I have described in detail in my work. It is the way in which the repressed and unreflected childhood biographies of parents and therapists influence the lives of children and patients entrusted to their care without anyone involved actually realizing it. At first glance, it may seem as if what goes on in cults and cultlike therapy groups takes place on a different level from the unconscious manipulation of children by their parents. We assume that in the former instance we are in the presence of an intentional, carefully planned, and organized form of manipulation aimed at exploiting the specific predicament of individuals.

In my view, however, this allegedly conscious exploitation can also be traced back to unconscious motives. Terrible as the consequences were, I do not believe, for example, that the two initiators of "feeling therapy," discussed earlier, actually set out to establish a totalitarian regime. It was the power they gained over their adherents that made them into gurus. And this is what I have in mind when I refer to the unconscious aspects of manipulation. In the end they themselves became the victims of a process with an inexorable logic of its own, a process they were unaware of because they had never given it any thought.

Thus they sparked off a conflagration they were unable to control, much less extinguish. First, they had learned how to reduce people to the emotional state of a helpless child. Once they had achieved that, they also learned how to use unconscious regression to exercise total control over their victims. From then on, what they did seemed to come automatically, in accordance with the child-rearing patterns instilled into them in their own childhood.

Mithers's report on the misleading blandishments that arouse false hopes and illusions also helps us to understand how political leaders operate. For years a debate has been raging on whether Hitler actually believed what he was saying or whether he consciously manipulated others. Was he a man obsessed with his self-appointed mission or a consummate actor, a Pied Piper luring millions to their doom? Some biographers have changed their minds on this point, tending more and more to the view that Hitler was indeed a fanatic believer in his own crazed doctrines. The question is a complex one, but one eminently worth following up because, as we see from the cult groups, it has lost none of its burning relevance for today.

If people stand up and proclaim they are prophets or agents of God, does that mean they are calculating charlatans, or are they lunatics genuinely believing they are in direct contact with Jesus? It is by no means easy to draw the line. In the case of "feeling therapy," it was clearly discernible how the craving for power engulfed any kind of realistic self-assessment on the part of the founders. They ended up believing they were as marvelous as their supporters thought them to be. They were asked to take part in 134 radio shows and 104 television programs. That

was enough to convince them that they were epoch-making
geniuses far superior to run-of-the-mill psychologists.

With cult leaders it is very difficult to say where the conscious ends and the unconscious begins. They are driven by
forces they are not aware of. If this were not the case, they
would not feel constrained to build up systems so intricate that
they can be maintained only by destructive means. With normal, conscious, systematic planning it would not be necessary
to proceed so elaborately. The gurus end up enmeshed in the
webs they have woven. The examples are legion. A case in
point, an extreme instance of pathological grandiosity, was the
mass murder in Jonestown, Guyana, in the late seventies. Others
followed suit. Common to all was the way in which mostly
well-meaning but misguided and confused people sacrificed
their own lives to salvage their belief in the sincerity of one obsessed individual—death as a means of preserving an illusion to
the bitter end.

Many of the people who establish cult groups are paranoid,
megalomaniac psychotics seeking protection from their own
anxieties in the mass of their adherents by passing themselves off
as helpers and healers. They proclaim that the end of the world is
nigh and build subterranean bunkers in an attempt to escape
their childhood feelings of helplessness and wage war on those
feelings at a symbolic level. At the same time they offer their services as saviors because that ensures them the adoration of their
disciples and enables them at last to feel powerful instead of
powerless and vulnerable, as they did in their childhood. But as
soon as they have grounds to fear exposure, they revert to threats
and coercion to force their followers to keep silence. Suicide is
the extreme form of self-imposed silence. It is also the course
elected by those thirty-nine young people who took their own
lives in a luxury villa in San Diego in 1997.

I do not believe that material greed alone is an adequate explanation for a system of fraud so elaborate as to inevitably involve unnecessary expenditure. The point is that it is not only the victims that lapse back into an infantile state, it is the people behind the system as well—be they little Hitlers or gurus. They bask in the admiration of their adherents, which they take to be a proof of their exceptional status and thus completely lose touch with reality. If this were not the case, Hitler would never have prolonged the Russian campaign in defiance of the advice of his experienced generals. But he was completely besotted with himself, a helpless victim of his own delusions of grandeur. His unconscious regression made him lose all contact with reality and any level-headed assessment of the situation.

Hitler, too, believed that the adulation of the masses was irrefutable evidence of his own greatness. The fact that this adulation was born of his own lies was something he could easily forget. Thus he came to regard himself as a genius. Like Hitler, gurus use paternal or maternal promises of healing and salvation to achieve complete and utter devotion. Regression without awareness, the total relapse into earliest infancy, is the instrument they use to blind the masses and keep them in a state of boundless adulation. This kind of regression makes criticism of parent figures like gurus and "charismatic" political leaders totally impossible. Equally inconceivable is self-criticism on the part of such leaders. It has no chance against the lust for power and the lure of self-aggrandisement.

Today, anyone who really wants to know how Hitler functioned need do no more than procure any tape of documentary footage on Hitler and watch it attentively. Observe the gestures and the facial expression of the Führer, listen to the sound of his ranting, euphoric voice, read the quotations from his speeches. Then the Hitler mystique will stop being such a mystique. It is

an example that can sharpen our perceptions and help us identify other, similar phenomena quickly and accurately.

For political leaders in the Hitler mold, the jubilation of the
masses is as indispensable to still their affective cravings as a drug
is for an addict. The millions of cheering supporters do not realize that they are needed for that purpose and that purpose alone.
When Hitler painted his glowing vision of a thousand-year
Reich free of revolutions, his listeners had no inkling whatever
that their beloved—and allegedly loving—father was getting
ready to send them off to their deaths in the war because his
own personal biography willed it so.

Some people are convinced that so-called deprogramming is
the best—indeed, the only—prospect of freeing cult group
members from their dependency and their psychological blindness. I for my part still believe in the power of information. If it
reaches people at the right moment, it can set off a process of reflection. Depending on the individual's personal situation, that
process of reflection will either be an ongoing process or it will
peter out. The effects may also be delayed, deferred until later.
The human mind is not a machine, an apparatus that can be re-
paired via outside agency. It has its own individual history, and
that history is the sole basis from which it can operate, the only
source for thought and action. Sometimes an emotional shock
will enable a person to wake up out of his regression and perceive reality as it is, even if that realization is a painful one.

WHAT IS HATRED?

ALTHOUGH CENTURIES OF NOVELS and autobiographies have dealt with the subject of child abuse in all its forms, society has been slow in recognizing the frequency with which this assault is committed. Only in the last twenty years has there been any real progress in this respect, and most of it is due to the efforts of a small number of researchers and above all to the media. Still underestimated and sometimes contested are the consequences very early abuse will have for the victims in their adult lives. The issues involved have been largely ignored by the scientific and academic community.

Even in certain therapeutic circles there is still controversy about the real significance of childhood experiences in the lives of adults. This was brought home to me by the correspondence I engaged in with an American adherent of Wilhelm Reich, who thought I was trying to belittle Reich's achievements by making reference to certain aspects of his biography. This was by no means my intention. On the contrary, I believe that today many therapists can profit from Reich's important discoveries, not least his work on the emotional armor with which the victims of early physical and mental cruelty or sexual abuse try to shield themselves.

But I was never able to agree with the concept of infantile sexuality that Reich adopted from Freud and developed further. Actually, in my book *Banished Knowledge,*[1] I advance the opinion that Freud masked the severe consequences of child abuse with his concept of infantile sexuality. I write: "Wilhelm Reich did the same thing later when he developed a theory intended to help him ward off the pain of the very young child he once was who had constantly been sexually exploited. Instead of feeling the hurt of being victimized by trusted adults and of having to accept his victimization submissively, Wilhelm Reich maintained throughout his life: I wanted that myself, I needed that, every child needs that!"

This statement is based on Myron Sharaf's biography of Reich,[2] according to which he reported that at the age of four he was privy to all the mysteries of sexual life, thanks to the initiation he received from a chambermaid who regularly took him to bed with her and gave him instruction in sex play. What I call sexual exploitation of a child's solitude may of course have been experienced differently from the child's viewpoint.

For Wilhelm Reich, it was almost certainly one of the things that rescued him in a time of despair, for example, when the mother he so loved committed suicide while he was still a child. He himself once said that the maid's bed had been a refuge for him. Understandably, this positive aspect blinded him to the fact that without his ever realizing it, he had been abused as an object of pleasure and a plaything.

Like any other form of exploitation practiced on children, sexual abuse may be accepted by the child as a kind of surrogate emotional nourishment if it has been starved of any other kind of affection. A child craving love, warmth, and protection may even avidly accept not only sexual interference but also blows, vilifications, and exaggerated demands if the only alternative is being rejected and abandoned altogether. I feel it is important for us not only to recognize and understand the illusions of infancy but also as adults to learn from the consequences of them. The denial of childhood suffering has far-reaching effects which are not limited to private family life but also play an operative role in major political upheavals and crises.

Children cannot understand why they should have injuries inflicted on them by the people they love and admire. They therefore reinterpret that behavior and believe it to be right. Cruelty is thus given a positive valuation in the child's cognitive system, and that valuation will be retained for life. Unless, that is, the child submits the whole process to a re-evaluation when he or she grows up.

Some people succeed in doing precisely that, either relatively early on in life or later. With this understanding, they will be able to leave the valuations of infancy behind and as adults acknowledge what was wrong, harmful, maybe even actively dangerous about the way their parents treated them. To do that, they first have to grow out of the state of childlike ignorance and helplessness. They no longer need to pretend that the beatings they were given did them good although precisely the opposite is the case.

But what happens if adults continue to steadfastly deny the harm they suffered, maintaining the infant position and glorifying the mistakes made by their parents? They may then end up condoning that violence as such, because they were given no opportunity of experiencing any alternatives and because the reasons for their parents' actions remain hidden from them. The destructive consequences may manifest themselves in adolescence in tyrannical treatment of younger siblings, in acts of violence, and possibly even murder.

Unfortunately, adults have some more methods at their disposal for denying the violence done to them in youth and taking that violence out on others. With sophisticated ideological justifications they can even contrive to pass it off as a good thing. The less inclination they show to recognize and revise this ingenious self-delusion, the more likely it is that others will be made to suffer the consequences. And it is this that ultimately confronts us with the apparent paradox of a nice, well-behaved child consummately skilled in living up to the adults' expectations and never voicing any criticism of them ending up thirty years later as a commandant in Auschwitz or as an Adolf Eichmann.

In all my books I have been concerned to demonstrate how the violence done to children devolves back on society as a whole. I was led to this conclusion by my inquiries into the way hatred develops, where it comes from. I wanted to find out why some people incline to extreme violence while others do not. Only when I started examining the childhood biographies of dictators and mass murderers[3] did I begin to understand. As children, all of them without exception were exposed to the horrors born of hypocrisy, and all of them ignored or denied the fact in later life. The atmosphere of hypocrisy they grew up in taught them to see cruelty as something good and useful. It was this denial that incited them to the retaliation campaigns they subsequently embarked on. A child battered and humiliated in the name of parental "care" will quickly internalize the language of violence and canting insincerity and come to see it as the only effective medium of communication.

In my work I have often referred to Hitler and Stalin as

graphic examples of the effects cruelty to children can have on society at large. In response, many people countered by saying that they had often been beaten themselves and that had not made war criminals out of them. Asked in more detail about their early years, they invariably disclosed that there had been at least one person who had shown them honesty, affection, or love, even though that person had not been able to protect them from physical mistreatment. This type of figure (I use the term "helping witness") can also be found in the biography of Dostoyevsky, who by all accounts had an extremely violent father but a loving mother. She passed on to her son the knowledge that such a thing as love actually exists, a knowledge without which his novels would have been unthinkable.

Among the victims of early cruelty, there are some who encounter not only helping witnesses of the more unconscious variety but also "knowing witnesses"—people who actively help them to recognize the wrong done to them for what it is and to articulate their sorrow at what has happened. Naturally enough, these children usually do not turn into violent criminals at a later stage. They are reasonably well aware of what they feel and what they do.

Studying child abuse confronts us with the astonishing fact that parents will inflict the same punishment or neglect on their children as they experienced themselves in their early lives. But as adults they have no recollection of what they went through. In the case of sexual assault on children, it is quite usual for the perpetrators to have no conscious knowledge of their own early life history or at the least to be cut off from the attendant feelings aroused by those experiences. It is not until they are in therapy—always supposing they are given any—that it transpires that they have been reenacting what they went through as children.

The sole explanation I can advance for this fact is that information on the cruelty suffered in childhood remains stored in the brain in the form of unconscious memories. For a child, conscious experience of such treatment is impossible. If children are not to break down completely under the pain and the fear, they must repress that knowledge. But the unconscious memories drive them to reproduce those repressed scenes over and over again in the vain attempt to liberate themselves from the fears that cruelty and abuse have left with them. Some victims create situations in which they can assume the active role in order to master the feeling of helplessness and escape the unconscious anxieties.

But this liberation is a specious one because the effects of the past don't change as long as they remain unnoticed. Repeatedly the perpetrator will go in search of new victims. As long as one projects hatred and fear onto scapegoats, there is no way of coming to terms with these feelings. Not until the cause has been recognized and the natural reaction to wrongdoing understood can the blind hatred wreaked on innocent victims be dissipated. The function it performs, that of masking the truth, is no longer necessary. There is evidence, as I cite in my preface, that sex criminals who have worked through their lives in therapy may no longer run the risk of a destructive reenactment of their traumas.

But what is hatred? As I see it, it is a possible consequence of the rage and despair that cannot be consciously felt by a child who has been neglected and maltreated even before he or she has learned to speak. As long as the anger directed at a parent or other first caregiver remains unconscious or disavowed, it cannot be dissipated. It can be taken out only on oneself or stand-ins, on scapegoats such as one's own children or alleged enemies. The variety of hatred that masquerades as righteous ideological zeal is particularly dangerous because its imperviousness to moral categories makes it unassailable. Sympathetic observation of the cries of an infant brings home forcibly to the onlooker how intense the feelings involved must be. The hatred can finally work as a life-saving defense against the life-threatening powerlessness.

An animal will respond to attack with "fight or flight." Neither course is open to an infant exposed to aggression from immediate family members. Thus the natural reaction remains pent up, sometimes for decades, until it can be taken out on a weaker object. Then these repressed emotions will be vented uninhibitedly on minorities. We call this xenophobia, and the victims differ from country to country—Turks, Sinti, Biafrans, Hutus, Tutsis, or whatever. In Mao's China it was the intellectuals. But the reasons for this hatred are the same everywhere.

Martin Luther, for example, was an intelligent and educated man, but he hated all Jews and he encouraged parents to beat their children. He was no perverted sadist, but four hundred years before Hitler he was disseminating this kind of destructive counsel. His mother had beaten him severely long before he was treated this way by his father and his teacher, and he believed this punishment had "done him good" and was therefore justified. The conviction stored in his body, that if parents do it then it must be right to torment someone weaker than yourself, left a much more lasting impression on him than the divine commandments and the Christian exhortations to love your neighbor and be compassionate toward the weak.

Similar cases are discussed by Philip Greven in his highly informative book *Spare the Child*.[4] He quotes various American men and women of the church recommending cruel beatings for babies and infants in the first few months of life as a way of ensuring that the lesson thus learned remains indelibly impressed on them for the rest of their lives. Unfortunately, they were only too right. These terrible destructive texts, which have misled so many parents, are the conclusive proof of the long-lasting effect of beating. They could have been written only by people who were exposed to merciless beatings as children and later glorified what they had been through.

We know that as a boy Hitler was tormented, humiliated, and mocked by his father, without his mother being able to protect him. We also know that he denied his true feelings toward his father. The real sources of his hatred thus become obvious.[5] I had gone in search of the true motives not only for Hitler's mental makeup but also for that of many other dictators. In all of them I identified the effects of hatred of at least one parent that remained unconscious. This hatred remained repressed because hating one's father was strictly prohibited, and because it was in the interests of the child's self-preservation to maintain the illusion of having a good father. Only in the form of a deflection onto others was hatred permitted, and then it could flow freely.

Hitler's specific problems with the Jews can in fact be traced back to the period before his birth. In her youth, his paternal grandmother had been employed in a Jewish merchant's household in Graz. After her return home to the Austrian village of Braunau, she gave birth to a son, Alois, later to become Hitler's father, and received child-support payments from the family in Graz for fourteen years. This story, which is recounted in many biographies of Hitler, represented a dilemma for the Hitler family. They had an interest in denying that the young woman had been left with child either by the Jewish merchant or his son. On the other hand, it was impossible to assert that a Jew would pay alimony for so long without good reason. Such generosity on the part of a Jew would have been inconceivable for the inhabitants of an Austrian village. Thus the Hitler family was faced with the insoluble dilemma of devising a version that would serve to nullify their "disgrace."

For Alois Hitler, the suspicion that he might be of Jewish descent was insufferable in the context of the anti-Jewish environment he grew up in. All the plaudits he himself earned as a customs officer were insufficient to liberate him from the latent rage at the disgrace and humiliation visited on him through no fault of his own. The only thing he could do with impunity was to take out this rage on his son Adolf. According to the reports of his daughter Angela, he beat his son mercilessly every day. In an attempt to exorcise his childhood fears, his son nurtured the maniac delusion that it was up to him to free not only himself of Jewish blood but also all Germany and later the whole world. Right up to his death in the bunker, Hitler remained a victim of this delusion because all his life his fear of his half-Jewish father had remained locked in his unconscious mind.

I have set out these ideas in greater detail in my book *For Your Own Good*. Many people have told me that they find them highly unsettling and in no way sufficient to explain Hitler's actions. Not all his actions, perhaps, but certainly his delusions. And those delusions are at the very least the foundation of his actions. I can certainly picture the boy Hitler swearing vengeance on "the Jews," those monstrous fantasy figures of an already diseased imagination. Consciously, he probably thought he could have led a happy life if "the Jew" had not plunged his grandmother into the disgrace that he and his family had to live with. And it was this that in his eyes served to excuse the batterings he received from his father, who after all was himself a victim of the evil and omnipotent Jew. In the mind of an angry, seriously confused child, it is only a short step from there to the idea that all Jews should be exterminated.

Not only Jews. In the household of Hitler's family lived for years the very unpredictable schizophrenic aunt Johanna whose behavior is reported to have been very frightening for the child. As an adult, Hitler ordered every handicapped and psychotic person to be killed, to free the German society from this burden. Germany seemed for him to symbolize the innocent child who had to be saved. Consequently, Hitler wanted to protect his nation from the dangers he himself had been faced with. Absurd? Not at all. For an unconscious mind, this kind of symbolization might sound very normal and logical.

Besides his fears in connection with his father and aunt, there was his early relationship with his very intimidated mother, who lived in constant fear of her husband's violent outbursts and beatings. She called him "oncle Alois" and endured patiently his humiliating treatment without any protest. Adolf's mother had lost the first three children due to an illness, and Adolf was her first child to survive infancy. We can easily imagine that the milk he received from his mother was in a way "poisoned" by her own fear. He drank her milk together with her fears but was, of course, unable to understand them or to integrate them. These irrational fears—that an outsider, watching his speeches on videos can easily recognize—stayed unrecognized and were unconscious to Hitler until the end of his life. Stored up in his body, they drove him constantly to new destructive actions, in his endless attempt to find a resolution.

In everyday language, the word *hatred* is also used to designate reactions that have nothing to do with deferred projections of infantile feelings onto scapegoats but with the justified anger felt by an adult in connection with a situation he or she is being forced to submit to. It is in this sense of the term that the victims of torture or the inmates of a labor camp can be said to "hate" their tormentors. This feeling frequently gives them the strength they need to survive; it protects them from resignation and enables them to preserve their dignity.

But this "hatred" is closely bound up with an actual, given situation. It is normally directed at persons radically interfering with our personal liberty, subjecting us to pain and humiliation not only in our imagination but in very real terms and making any kind of expression impossible. If such victims are able to extricate themselves from that situation and get away from their tormentors, this anger may get weaker in the course of time and possibly even disappear altogether.

Not so in the case of Hitler, Stalin, Mao, and other dictators driven by hatred until the very hour of their deaths, although as adults they had no reason to be. On the contrary, they were revered and adulated by millions, and they had no reason to feel any anxiety beyond what they had preserved from their childhood. But that anxiety fueled their hatred all their lives.

In the lives of all the tyrants I examined, I found without exception paranoid trains of thought bound up with their biographies in early youth and the repression of the experiences they had been through. Mao sent 30 million people to their deaths, but he never fully admitted the extent of the rage he felt for his own father. Stalin caused millions to suffer and die because even at the height of his power, his actions were determined by unconscious infantile fear of powerlessness. Apparently, his father, a poor cobbler from Georgia, attempted to drown his frustration with liquor and whipped his son almost every day. His mother displayed psychotic traits, was completely incapable of defending her son, and was usually away from home either praying in church or running the priest's household. Stalin idealized his parents right up to the end of his life and was constantly haunted by the fear of dangers that had long since ceased to exist but were still present in his deranged mind.

The same is true of many other tyrants. The groups of people they singled out for persecution and the rationalization mechanisms they employed were different in each case, but the fundamental reason behind it was similar. They often drew on ideologies to disguise the truth and their own paranoia. And the masses chimed in enthusiastically because they were unaware of the real motives, including those operative in their own biographies. The infantile revenge fantasies of individuals would be of no account if society did not regularly show such naive alacrity in helping to make them come true.

As there has so far been little scientific inquiry into the effects of early cruelty on the later lives of the victims, there is correspondingly little mention of them in historical and anthropological studies. Thus sociologist Wolfgang Sovsky is able to write an otherwise impressive work on forms of violence[6] without making one single reference to the childhood dimension. He gives very considerable space to the willful infliction of suffering, calling it "mysterious" although it is readily explicable once we countenance the idea that executioners, torturers, and the orchestrators of organized manhunts may have learned their fateful lessons very early. It is a well-known fact that things learned early in life are extremely hard to dislodge; in the course of time they can become "second nature."

This does not of course exonerate the perpetrators of such criminal deeds. But it should motivate us to seriously consider the hypothesis that the propensity for active and voluntary involvement in organized genocide and torture is not a quirk of nature, an "act of God." The individuals displaying such inclinations belong to the sizable group of people who have never developed the capacity to feel pity and compassion, or else have forfeited that capacity very early. The brains of these people may otherwise function impeccably, and this coupled with their crippling deficits in the emotional sphere make them ideal instruments for the implementation of the crazed designs of paranoid leaders.

Of course, there are people who have not turned into murderers or child molesters, although they themselves were severely mistreated in childhood. But I myself have yet to come across a criminal of that kind who was not a victim as a child. The problem is that most of these people are unaware of their motives; they have no access to their feelings and memories. Daniel J. Goldhagen's book[7] is based largely on testimonies of perpetrators. This approach enables him to cast light on the emotional lives of these people and make them accessible to further study. The quotations and the picture material establish beyond all doubt that the expressions of satisfaction and enjoyment on the faces of the tormentors are a true reflection of the pleasure they took in killing and maiming.

Unfortunately, Goldhagen restricts himself to a phenomenological discussion of the people who volunteered to torture and humiliate others. He does not give any consideration to their childhoods. He devotes much attention to the emotions of the perpetrators, a subject hitherto largely ignored, but without the background of their early upbringing, their behavior still remains mysterious. The reader seeks in vain for an explanation. What made respected members of society suddenly act like monsters? How can a former teacher like Klaus Barbie and other men described by their daughters as kind, caring fathers, have innocent people tortured or indeed do the torturing themselves? Goldhagen does not address this question. He is obviously convinced that references to traditional anti-Semitism in Germany provide a satisfactory answer. They do not.

The hypothesis that German anti-Semitism was the real reason for the Holocaust has been rightly criticized by urging a

comparison with the First World War. At that time, anti-
Semitism was just as strong in Germany but no organized genocide resulted. And why no Holocaust in the other anti-Semitic
countries—Poland, Russia, and other parts of Europe? The
argument that in the Weimar Republic unemployment and
poverty caused immense general frustration that was discharged
via the mass murder of the Jews is hardly convincing, given that
Hitler was quickly successful in getting unemployment under
control.

There were other factors at play that have hitherto been
ignored, factors going some way to explaining why the Holocaust happened in Germany and why it happened at this particular time rather than another. In my view, the operative
factor is definitely the destructive child-rearing style practiced
widely on infants around the turn of the century in Germany,
a style I have no hesitation in referring to as a universal abuse
of infants.

Of course, children in other countries have been and still are
mistreated in the name of upbringing or caregiving, but hardly
with the systematic thoroughness characteristic of the so-called
Poisonous Pedagogy (Schwarze Pädagogik). In the two generations before Hitler's rise to power, the implementation of this
method was brought to a high degree of perfection in Germany.
With this foundation to build on, Hitler finally achieved what he
wanted: "My ideal of education is hard. Whatever is weak must
be hammered away. In the fortresses of my militant order, a generation of young people will grow to strike fear into the heart of
the world. Violent, masterful, unafraid, cruel youth is what I
want. Young people must be all that. They must withstand pain.
There must be nothing weak or tender about them. The free,
magnificent predator must flash from their eyes again. I want
them strong and beautiful. That way I can fashion things anew."

This education program revolving on the extermination of everything life-giving was the forerunner of Hitler's plans for the extermination of an entire nation. Indeed, it was the prerequisite for the ultimate success of his designs.

The numerous and widely read tracts by Dr. Daniel Gottlieb Moritz Schreber, the inventor of the *Schrebergärten* (the German word for small allotments) are of major interest here. Some of them ran to as many as forty editions, and their central concern was to instruct parents in the systematic upbringing of infants from the very first day of life. Many people, motivated by what they thought to be the best of intentions, complied with the advice given them by Schreber and other authors about how best to raise their children if they wanted to make them into model subjects of the German Reich. They did this without even remotely suspecting that they were exposing their children to a systematic form of torture with long-term effects. German sayings and catchphrases, like "Praise be to the things that make us tough" and "What doesn't kill us will strengthen us," still to be heard from educationists of the old school, probably originated in this period.

Morton Schatzman,[8] who quotes highly enlightening passages from Schreber's writings, is of the opinion that here we are in the presence not of child-rearing methods but of systematic instruction in child persecution. One of Schreber's convictions is that when babies cry, they should be made to desist by the use of "physically perceptible admonitions," assuring his readers that "such a procedure is only necessary once, or at the most twice, and then one is master of the child for all time. From then on, one look, one single threatening gesture will suffice to subjugate the child." Above all, the newborn child should be drilled from the very first day to obey and to refrain from crying.

Today, people who have been brought up in anything even remotely approaching a humane way will hardly be able to imagine the rigor and tenacity with which Schreber himself implemented this program. Psychoanalyst Wilhelm G. Niederland[9] quotes examples that cast light on the everyday practical conduct of child-rearing in those decades, for example, recipes for inculcating the "art of self-denial" into infants: "The method should be simple and effective: the child is placed on the lap of its nanny while the latter is eating or drinking whatever takes her fancy. However urgent the infant's oral needs may become in this situation, they must not be gratified."

Niederland (p. 98) quotes an account by Schreber from his own family life. A nanny eating pears while holding one of his children on her lap was unable to resist the temptation of giving the infant a slice. She was immediately dismissed. The news of this draconian measure quickly spread to all the other nannies in Leipzig, and from that time on, writes Schreber, he "never again encountered such insubordination, neither with that child nor with any of the others that came later."

Contrary to received opinion prevalent only a few years ago, the human brain at birth is not fully developed. The abilities a person's brain develops depend on experiences in the first three years of life. Studies on abandoned and severely mistreated Romanian children revealed striking lesions in certain areas of the brain and marked emotional and cognitive insufficiencies in later life. According to very recent neurobiological findings, repeated traumatization leads to an increased release of stress hormones that attack the sensitive tissue of the brain and destroy existing neurons. Other studies of mistreated children have revealed that the areas of the brain responsible for the "management" of the emotions are 20 to 30 percent smaller than in normal persons.

The children systematically subjected to obedience drills

around the turn of the century were exposed not only to corporal "correction" but also to severe emotional deprivation. The upbringing manuals of the day described physical demonstrations of affection, such as stroking, cuddling, and kissing, as indications of a doting, mollycoddling attitude. Parents were warned of the disastrous effects of spoiling their children, a form of indulgence entirely incompatible with the prevalent ideal of rigor and severity. As a result, infants suffered from the absence of direct loving contact with the parents. The best they could hope for was to find some kind of substitute from the servants, who in numerous cases used and exploited them as objects of pleasure, thus frequently adding to the children's emotional confusion.

Since the experiments conducted on monkeys by Dr. Harlow in the fifties, we know that animals raised by artificial "robot" mothers later turned aggressive and showed no interest in their own offspring. John Bowlby's studies on the absence of early attachment in delinquents and René Spitz's descriptions of small children dying of hospitalism, emotional neglect during hospitalization under extremely hygienic conditions, are indications that not only animal but also human babies require reassuring sensory contact with their parents if socialization is to take a normal course.

These findings presented by Bowlby and Spitz many years ago are corroborated by recent neurobiological research. The studies in question suggest that not only active battering but also the absence of loving physical contact between child and parent will cause certain areas of the brain, notably those responsible for the emotions, to remain underdeveloped. Hence the children "subjugated by looks" suffered emotional harm that was only to develop its full destructive potential in the next generation.

Present-day neurobiological research makes it easier for us to understand the way Nazis like Eichmann, Himmler, Höss, and others functioned. The rigorous obedience training they underwent in earliest infancy stunted the development of such human capacities as compassion and pity for the sufferings of others. They were incapable of emotion in the face of misfortune (as documented in my book *For Your Own Good);* such feelings were alien to them. What Himmler called "freedom" in his famous speech in Poznan was in fact total emotional atrophy. It enabled the perpetrators of the most heinous crimes imaginable to function "normally" and to continue to impress their environment with their efficiency in the years after the war. Without the slightest remorse, Dr. Mengele could make the most cruel experiments on Jewish children in Auschwitz and then live for thirty years as a normal well-adjusted man.

This latter phenomenon remains a mystery that resists anything approaching a satisfactory explanation. But even if we had such an explanation, we would still be unable to prevent the "production" of such individuals, quite simply because the practice of child-rearing is so slow to respond to the findings of scientific research. Whether these latest insights ever in fact reach young parents depends in the first instance on their emotional maturity, a conclusion that Daniel and Claudia come to in my story. Happily, there are already many young parents, like Anna and Robert or Mary and Ralph in the story "Yolanta and Linda," who despite their youth have achieved this maturity.

Many parents of the younger generation are no longer intimidated by the advice of people who, because they were beaten as children, continue to assert that a slap at the "right moment" will do a child "a power of good" and certainly no lasting harm. Young parents with an affectionate attachment to their children are sometimes better informed on this point than members of the medical community. They know that a child must never be beaten because the blows inflicted can have the effect of an emotional time bomb. Those effects may manifest themselves much later, even if "only" in the form of educated people still going around recommending such barbarity in the face of all the hard facts that speak against it.

In the 1970s, Sweden enacted legislation prohibiting the use of physical force on children. At the time, 70 percent of the citizens questioned in surveys were against the idea. Today that figure is down to 10 percent. New experiences have obviously opened many people's eyes. In the larger European countries it is still unfortunately permissible to "discipline" young children with strokes of the cane, to make sure they turn into "useful members of society," whatever that may mean. Canes for that purpose are still produced in France, and sales figures are high.

An awareness of the damage done to the emotional constitution of children by mental cruelty, psychological and physical deprivation, mistreatment in infancy, and the suppression of emotional responses makes it easier to understand why these suppressed emotions generate a strong desire for revenge. It is thus only logical to assume that thrity or forty years later they will be abreacted in contexts and situations where this is not only permitted but actively encouraged.

The question of why some people survive cruelty without any apparent impairments while others develop severe physical symptoms or turn criminal can perhaps be answered only in individual cases, and not always even then. But there can be no doubt that the presence of one or more compassionate persons in early youth will facilitate a positive development despite occasional traumatic experiences because this makes it possible to identify and reject cruelty as such and consciously come to terms with it.

In this connection it would of course be possible to argue along the same lines as Freud's approach to sexuality and say that if the majority of people have been battered, abused, molested, or emotionally neglected as children, then this cannot be a pathogenic factor leading to delinquency; if it were, most people would be murderers. But this argument fails to engage with the fact that it is not the traumas themselves that generate neuroses and set people off on careers of crime but the way individual people process them.

In the absence of positive factors, affection, and helping witnesses, the only course open to the mistreated individual seems to be the disavowal of personal suffering and the idealization of cruelty with all its devastating aftereffects. Undergoing an exceedingly humiliating and cruel upbringing at the preverbal stage, usually without helping witnesses, may instill into the victim admiration of this cruelty if there is no one in the immediate vicinity of the child to query those methods and stand up for humane values.

Extensive passages of my book *For Your Own Good* are given over to quoting extracts from education journals from the beginning of the century. This is designed to bring home to the reader how infants were tormented, not to say tortured, physically and mentally, on the assumption that this would be good for their characters. A psychoanalyst friend of mine, who has since died, read them in manuscript form. She said that after ten pages she could no longer bear to go on and was so furious that she hurled the manuscript against the wall. The texts had triggered vivid memories of the way she herself had been raised. She was not normally given to such outbursts, but the texts had rekindled the helpless rage of the tormented child, the rage that she had repressed all those years. Later, when she had read the whole book, she called her grandparents "Schreber children" and understood where her parents had inherited the terrible array of punishments that caused her so much torment.

I asked myself what goes on in the mind of a small child forced to submit to those tortures perpetrated in the name of a crazed idea and unable to defend herself against them. Dr. Schreber had two sons. One of them committed suicide; the other developed a psychosis. But not all children subjected to such child-rearing doctrines suffered similar fates, so it seems fair to assume that not all parents complied with those tenets. Other children, like my friend, had helping witnesses, thanks to whom they never entertained the aberration that the treatment meted out to them had done them good. But a large remainder grew up believing that tormenting, humiliating, and mocking children serves a high moral purpose and must be borne in obedience and humility.

As the example of Luther shows, nothing that a child learns later about morality at home, in school, or in church will ever have the same effect as the treatment inflicted on his or her body in the first few days, weeks, and months. The lesson learned in the first three years cannot be expunged. If the body of a child learns from birth that tormenting and punishing an innocent creature is the right thing to do, that message will always be stronger than intellectual knowledge acquired at a later stage. Greven's examples eloquently demonstrate that people subjected to mistreatment in childhood may go on insisting all their lives that beatings are harmless and corporal punishment is salutary, although there is overwhelming, indeed conclusive, evidence to the contrary. Vice versa, a child protected, loved, and cherished from the outset will thrive on that experience for a lifetime.

What do we know today about the female "kapos," those women who had so openly and unreservedly relished the job of tormenting and humiliating Jewish children and subjecting them to every conceivable variety of mental and physical cruelty. The trial records revealed that most of them were young women between nineteen and twenty-one who had formerly had quite ordinary jobs as seamstresses or sales clerks and whose biographies contained nothing in any way unusual. During the trial, they unanimously claimed that they had not been aware that Jewish children were human beings. The conclusion that immediately suggests itself is that ultimately propaganda and manipulation are sufficient to transform people into sadistic executioners and mass murderers.

This is not an opinion I share. On the contrary. It is my belief that only men and women who had experienced mental and physical cruelty in the first weeks and months of life and had been shown no love at all could possibly have let themselves be made into Hitler's willing executioners. As Goldhagen's archive material shows, they needed next to no ideological indoctrination because their bodies knew exactly what they wanted to do as soon as they were allowed to follow their inclinations. And as the Jews, young or old, had been declared nonpersons, there was nothing to stop them from indulging those inclinations. But no amount of indoctrination alone will unleash hatred in a person who has no predisposition in that direction. There were also Germans, like Karl Jaspers, Hermann Hesse, or Thomas Mann, who immediately recognized the declaration that Jews were nonpersons as an alarm signal and the rallying cry of untrammeled barbarism.

For people like the *blokowas,* exposed to emotional confusion in their early childhood, the declaration was a highly convenient expedient. All they needed to do was refuse the children water to wash themselves, and that gave them sufficient reason to hate them for being dirty and coal black. They could toss lumps of sugar to starving children and then despise them for the alacrity with which they scrambled to pick them up. Those young women could turn the children into precisely what they needed to feel powerful and could thus vent on their victims the old, unconscious rage slumbering within them. I feel that it is futile to speculate how many Austrian belonged to the SS. Luckily, in present-day Austria, beating children is forbidden by law. This justifies the hope that in the next generations only a minority will be prepared to perpetrate deeds that in earlier times the majority may have been willing to commit.

The studies at my disposal already in 1980 and referred to in *For Your Own Good* confirmed my conjecture that, both in Nazi Germany and among the professional American soldiers who volunteered in Vietnam, brutally raised children figured prominently among the most vindictive war criminals. Further confirmation was brought by study of the childhood biographies of those exceptional people who in times of terror had the courage to rescue others from extermination.·

Why were there people brave enough to risk their lives to save Jews from Nazi persecution? Much scientific inquiry has been expended on this question. The usual answers revolve around religious or moral values such as Christian charity or a sense of responsibility instilled in them by parents, teachers, and other caregivers. But there is no doubt that the active supporters of the extermination drive and the passive hangers-on had usually also been given a religious upbringing. So this can hardly furnish a sufficient explanation.

I was convinced that there must have been some special factor in the childhood of the rescuers, in the prevailing atmosphere of their childhood, that made it so fundamentally different from what the war criminals had experienced. For years I sought in vain for a book that would give this subject adequate coverage. Finally, I chanced on an empirical study[10] based on interviews with more than four hundred witnesses of those dark days. It confirmed my hypothesis. The study concluded that the only factor distinguishing the rescuers from the persecutors and hangers-on was the *way* they had been brought up by their parents.

Almost all rescuers interviewed reported that their parents had attempted to discipline them with arguments rather than punishment. They were only rarely subjected to corporal punishment, and if they were, it was invariably in connection with some misdemeanor and never because their parents had felt the need to discharge some uncontrollable and inexplicable feeling of rage on them. One man recalled that he had once been spanked for taking smaller children out onto a frozen lake and endangering their lives. Another reported that his father had hit him only once and apologized afterward. Many of the statements might be paraphrased thus: "My mother always tried to explain what was wrong about whatever it was I had done. My father also spent a lot of time talking to me. I was impressed by what he had to say."

What a different picture we get from the reports of the persecutors and hangers-on: "When my father was drunk, he took the whip to me. I never knew what I was being beaten for. Often it was for something I had done months before. And when mother was in a temper, she tore into anyone who got in her way, including me."

Unlike such uncontrolled affective discharges subjectively felt to be justified, explaining what the parent feels is wrong is synonymous with trust in the otherwise good intentions of the child. Such a course is motivated by respect and faith in the child's ability to develop and change his or her behavior for the better.

People given early affection and support are quick to emulate the sympathetic and autonomous natures of their parents. Common to all the rescuers were self-confidence, the ability to make immediate decisions, and the capacity for empathy and compassion with others. Seventy percent of them said that it took them only a matter of minutes to decide they wanted to intervene. Eighty percent said they did not consult anyone else: "I had to do it. I could never have stood idle and watched injustice being done."

This attitude, prized in all cultures as "noble," is not something instilled in children with fine words. If the behavior actually displayed by caretakers is such as to contradict their own words, if children are spanked in the name of lofty ideals, as is still the custom in some parochial schools, then those elevated sentiments are doomed to go unheard or even to provoke rage and violence. The children may end up aping those high-minded phrases and mouthing them in later life, but they will never put them into practice because they have no example to emulate.

Punishment is meted out on the assumption that a child has acted with willful malice. No wonder that the result is not trust but fear. The child learns that the strong have the right to make arbitrary use of their power. Children brought up on violence without a helping witness are afraid of new experiences because everywhere they sense the lurking danger of suddenly being punished for alleged misbehavior. As adults they are forced to navigate their way through life without the compass of experience to guide them. For that reason, they will kowtow to authority and persecute those weaker than themselves, just as they were exposed to the arbitrary exercise of power by their caregivers when they were young.

Even in the sinister years of the Third Reich there were isolated individuals whose ingrained moral rejection of cruelty was firmly rooted in their early emotional lives. I have illustrated the point elsewhere with reference to the resistance fighter Sophie Scholl. The upbringing she had been given was very different from the prevalent patterns of the day in Germany. Her home background was imbued with a spirit of kindness and generosity. Thus, even as a girl, Sophie was immune to the blandishments of Hitler's ideologies. His speeches filled her with revulsion.

Today Sophie Scholl would no longer be an exception. This fact may perhaps give us grounds to hope that in present-day Germany it would not be so easy to organize full-scale genocide without resistance from the people. There might be a likelihood of minority groups chiming in with such ravings because all over the world, and not only in Germany, there are young people ready and waiting to avenge the humiliations inflicted on them by taking their pent-up rage and frustration out on others. But despite unemployment and general dissatisfaction with successive governments, I can hardly imagine a majority of German citizens falling in with the rantings of a maniac politician openly advertising his intention to create order by exterminating a whole nation.

Generally speaking, there can be no doubt that today German children are given a different and much freer upbringing than the kind practiced on their grandparents in the early 20th century. What the majority was exposed to then is limited to a minority today. I base this conclusion on a number of indicators, including the fact that the strongest postwar pacifist movement was to be found in Germany and that in spite of some weaknesses, democracy has firmly established itself there. This gives us grounds for optimism. The question of what triggered this positive development has hardly been addressed, let alone answered. I feel sure that a liberalization of child-rearing methods is one of the factors involved. How did this liberalization come about?

Time alone will not bring about such a development. In Russia, various revolutions and two world wars have not been sufficient to unsettle the antiquated upbringing methods still largely subscribed to, fortunately without any kind of system. It may well be that in Germany the shock of the postwar years played a part in making upbringing methods less rigorous. Nor is it inconceivable that, despite emotional resistance or even hatred toward the American forces, their presence may have contributed to undermining a mentality based on servility to authority. These two factors may have been mutually supportive and may also have been reinforced by a number of others.

In Germany and elsewhere in Europe, the reason for the increase in juvenile violence is seen in the sentence offered to young offenders. But anyone taking a true interest in the question will be quick to recognize that in fact it is exposure to extreme physical correction, abuse, or neglect in childhood that turns out young adults who take pleasure in destruction and who worship violence.

Despite the serious demonstrable harm done to the brain by physical abuse in the first three years, it is perhaps never too late to help the youthful victim to develop a trusting attitude if his environment shows the necessary understanding. The human brain is infinitely inventive. Under ideal conditions it appears to be able to activate other regions to function as a substitute for those areas it has forfeited. The successes registered by circumspect therapists and humane instructors are a proof of this. But the indispensable precondition is that the harm done be identified as such, not disavowed or played down. In some cases, a confrontation with the past appears to me unavoidable if we want to change things for the better and thus accept our share of the responsibility for the future.

In a newspaper interview,[11] a German professor was asked for his views on the fact that, after the war, most university professors who had been supporters of the Nazi regime did not own up to their involvement. The professor had served in the SS as a young man and had been decorated for valiant service on the eastern front. He interpreted this silence as a sign of shame. Some things, he said, are so atrocious that it is best not to talk about them. One should not try to understand what is beyond all understanding.

Whether the real motive was indeed shame and not opportunism is a moot point. At all events, this kind of distancing from the past seems to me extremely problematic in that it involves a danger of repetition on the grounds of sheer ignorance. In my opinion, it is important for us to gain a precise understanding of how such atrocities could come about, to find out exactly why so many intellectuals gave them their unconditional approval, and why they still refuse to make an honest effort to understand what happened to them. And *why* it happened to them.

Naturally, for some readers, my references to Schreber and his methods will not be sufficient to explain the history of the Holocaust. Countless books have been written about it, but the enormity of those crimes still defies comprehension. Blaming the whole thing on a defective genetic blueprint is just as unsatisfactory. Why should there have been so many people born thirty or forty years before the Holocaust in Germany with such a fateful genetic disposition? I don't know of any gene researcher who has tried to answer this question.

My references to the systematic humiliation of children around the turn of the century and the torture they were exposed to (tragically, never recognized as such by the parents) contain the crucial factor that explains such barbarity. Unfortunately, it has yet to be given the attention it deserves. The reasons for this neglect are probably closely connected with the general taboo that has been imposed on the subject of childhood. But for quite hardheaded pragmatic reasons, notably a concern for the future, it is important to break with this taboo and venture onto this largely unexplored territory.

The total neglect or trivialization of the childhood factor operative in the context of violence and the way it evolves sometimes leads to explanations that are not only unconvincing and abortive but actively deflect attention away from the genuine roots of violence. The abstract term "anti-Semitism" contains an infinite number of meanings and frequently serves only to blur the complicated psychological processes involved, processes that need to be identified and called by name. This is the only way we can hope to change anything.

The reasons for various instances of genocide have by no means been established beyond all doubt. It would be worthwhile to study the upbringing principles of various peoples (for example, in Africa, Asia, and Australia) that see their only salvation in the extermination of other peoples. The psychological background for the extermination of the Native Americans is antoher issue that has yet to be adequately investigated. The Native Americans themselves have only just started inquiring into the problem.

In my view, a close comparison of parenting methods today and in the past can bring about such a change. It can open up new vistas and encourage the formation of new and healthier structures in raising children. Many new enlightening books on parent-child relations are instances of concrete help for parents in incorporating the information at our disposal into the practice of child-rearing. Parents following such advice are likely to find it easier to respect, encourage, understand, and love their children. But working toward a better, more aware future cannot be done in isolation from the ongoing attempt to understand our history, as individuals and as society, in all its facets. One of those facets, the history of child-rearing, seems to me more eloquent than any other in illustrating the dangers for society at large, attendant on willful ignorance about child development.

Afterword

WE HAVE FINALLY ARRIVED at a general consensus that mistreatment of children is a bad thing. But many people are unaware of the fact that physical "correction" of any kind, including spanking, is invariably synonymous with mistreatment. All over the world this fact is held to be axiomatic as far as full-grown adults are concerned, but when defenseless children are involved, the case is apparently not so clear-cut. This double standard could survive unscathed only as long as beating one's children, so-called corporal punishment, was passed off as a licit method of "licking them into shape" or "hammering some sense into them." The consequences of such treatment—and it is no exaggeration to say that genocide and the toleration of genocide is one of them—have simply been ignored. It is one of the most tragic instances of miscommunication in the history of the world. From one generation to the next, this inhuman method of bringing up children has been applied and accepted as "God-given." "It's for your own good," the parents say, and their children believe it and do the same thing to their children. And this has been going on for centuries.

However, in the face of approaching death, some old people are reviewing their whole lives, undergoing a stock-taking process. What could be more important for them than to engage with all those unanswered questions in the company of their children? Talking things over means looking each other in the eye, exchanging arguments. It becomes possible to admit to one-self and to one's own children: No, beating never did any good; it harmed us all; it distorted our lives and minds.

Such simple words, which have the same meaning for every generation, might put an end to decades of deceit and self-deceit. Furthermore, they might go some way to correcting the errors committed simply by conceding them to be errors and thus liberating themselves of guilt feelings, which are no less operative for being unconscious. Why are these words so rarely uttered? Maybe the reason some young people say nothing has less to do with their own personal fears than with the affection they feel for their parents, which makes them want to humor their anxieties and taboos instead of helping them to free themselves. But sparing the parents' feelings by remaining silent only widens the gulf. This is not necessary, not anymore. By talking to their parents, they could give them a precious gift, the gift of truth. And the truth, even if it comes late in life, can still change that life for the better.

Giving this truth a place in our lives means letting it point the way to action that we may not have dared to envisage before. People in high places could support new legislation ensuring that in the future, children will be spared barbarity in all its forms, and especially corporal punishment. Today, this kind of process could be initiated by people who have never been beaten themselves, or by others who although they were not spared that fate have recognized, thanks to the sympathy of others, what a shadow this cruelty has cast on their previous lives. As they are no longer children themselves, and can argue cogently for the cause they are championing, they do not need to fear defense mechanisms on the part of others. As adults able to come to terms with reality in all its forms, they will be able to cope with those mechanisms, as well.

In the recent past, young people have gone into the streets to demonstrate for all kinds of good causes, against war, for protection of the environment, and above all for more humanity. But there have never been any demonstrations supporting the right of children not to be beaten by their caregivers. Why not? I wonder. Why have we been so slow to realize that many of the instances of violence that we campaign against have their sources in the cradle and the playroom? And that we can prevent further acts of violence only by condemning that first devastating experience of violence right at the beginning of a child's life?

Today, we know this. There are very few things we can be so absolutely sure about. We know beyond any doubt that beating children has only detrimental effects; it is disastrous for the self-respect both of the victim and the perpetrator. And it teaches children misleading lessons, for example, that a child doesn't deserve respect, that a child's feelings of pain should be ignored or minimized, and that it is the victim who should feel guilty. Every generation can play a role in spreading the right knowledge. Every individual, whether grandchild or grandparent, regardless of origins and social status, can do his or her part to make sure that it establishes itself as an acknowledged fact of life, both in the family and in the immediate environment.

All we need to ask of ourselves is to speak out, whenever the opportunity presents itself, or at least to stop asserting that beating did us good, that we deserved it, and so forth. Such statements have spread enough confusion in the course of history and brought a great deal of damage into the bargain. The only conceivable reason for maintaining such assertions is the desire to disavow our own suffering. But we must not allow ourselves to uphold that denial at the expense of society. If we do, it will fall back on our own heads.

We live in an age of unemployment; we are witnesses to the return of mass superstition, the commercialization of emotional problems, the triumph of cult groups. All that and much more might seem reason enough to be pessimistic. But we also live in an age where more young people than ever before are growing up free of the bane of physical mistreatment. I see this as a genuine cause for optimism. Thanks to their own personal experience, these people can help to counteract a destructive tradition that has contributed to the proliferation of violence for thousands of years. They are adequately equipped to resist resignation and pessimism and to take advantage of the real opportunities for change that present themselves.

Turning away from the truth will never help us preserve love, and the love we have for our parents is no exception. The act of forgiveness will not help as long as it serves to disguise the facts. For love and self-delusion are mutually exclusive. The disavowal of truth, the denial of the sufferings we have been through, is the breeding ground for the kind of hatred that gets deflected onto innocent victims. It is an act of self-deception and an impasse from which there is no way out. Genuine love can face up to the truth.

Postscript

REVISING THIS BOOK for the paperback edition, I have decided to omit one of the case studies after receiving from its protagonist an account of the way her story has developed in the meantime. In the hardcover version of *Paths of Life* (1998), a grown-up daughter, whom I call Sandra, proudly relates that she has succeeded in persuading herself to visit her elderly father and, with relative equanimity, to confront him with the fact that he abused her sexually when she was small. She was proud that she had not allowed herself to be swamped by strong feelings and had calmly told him about what she had found out in the course of therapy. As her father could not deny these facts, Sandra felt confident that she could look forward to a complete recovery from her residual symptoms. But to her amazement, these symptoms actually became more acute in the space of only a few years. At the same time, new memories and distressing dreams assailed her, revealing her father's extreme sadism, which she had been unaware of up to that point. She now realized that her father's jovial "confession" had deceived her about the *whole* truth, and this realization provoked a towering rage in her. It was the rage of a small girl at her omnipotent father, who had sacrificed her at such an early stage to his pedophiliac leanings. The intense feelings, dreams, and physical responses aroused by all this revealed that this man had nothing to do with the well-meaning father who had so easily confessed to his abusive behavior when she met him in Toronto. At that meeting he must have known that Sandra's memories revealed only part of the truth. So he continued to play the part of the nice, rather patronizing daddy whose sincerity she so dearly wanted to believe in. Only now did she realize that he had left no trace of empathy for his little child in her memory.

It was this long pent-up, immeasurable rage that freed the adult Sandra from her idealization of her father and her "love" for him. At long last she was able to relinquish the compassion she had cultivated within herself since her childhood as a token of her own generosity. She could finally perceive the full extent of the cruelty done to her as a child, and her migraine attacks and insomnia disappeared as a result.

My book *Paths of Life* was already in the bookshops when I heard of the turn these events had taken. In the meantime, the reader mail addressed to my website has shown me that many women are unable to sever the bonds attaching them to their fathers, though they are clear in their minds about the brutality with which they were beaten and humiliated. Some of them even suffer from multiple sclerosis or fibromyalgia, chronic pain disorders indicating the beatings they received from their parents and suppressed rage during childhood. Yet they still adhere unswervingly to the conviction that they love their parents and are loved by them in return. In childhood, acceptance and expression of that rage would have involved severe punishment or total abandonment, and the fear of these consequences lives on in the adult children. But as soon as they realize that they are no longer in danger, they will be able to understand the situation they were in as children and to rebel inwardly against the cruelties perpetrated on them, instead of continuing to forgive them "generously." Normally, this will bring relief, and the body will no longer need to avail itself of the symptoms that are its only way of expressing itself.

I soon realized that Sandra's wishes had deceived me into thinking—like many therapists—that a "beneficial" heart-to-heart talk with the parents can help to alleviate the injuries inflicted in childhood. Today, years later, I doubt that this is true. Even if Sandra's father had "come clean," even if he had sincerely admitted to his sadistic games (and this rarely, if ever, happens), he could still not have relieved her of the work she had to do. In my latest book[1] I describe this "work" and the inner processes it involves. The reality of childhood will never go away. Even if these parents were all suddenly transformed into angels, the memories of their cruelties, their hatred, and their rejection remain as knowledge stored in the bodies of their children. The task devolving on the adult children is to free themselves of those memories, not by forgiving and forgetting, but by accepting the logical response to torture, the experience of rage they have denied themselves for so long. Medication can do nothing to reveal this truth. All it can do is to camouflage it, often for decades, without bringing any genuine relief.

Like Sandra, most of us are adamant in refusing to believe that parents can be so cruel to their little, innocent children, despite the appalling facts we read about in the papers every day.

This refusal leads to a deceptive idealization of our own child-hood and hence to an unconscious repetition of that cruelty. The only thing that can help us to relinquish our blindness and spare our children the same fate is the courage to accept this truth.

Notes

Introduction

1. Gillen David, ed., *J'ai commis l'inceste*. Edition de l'Homme, 1995.

Claudia and Daniel

1. Françoise Dolto, *Solitude*. Paris: Vestige, 1982.
2. Ashley Montagu, *Touching: The Human Significance of the Skin*. New York: Harper & Row, 1971.
3. "Your Child from Birth to Three," *Newsweek,* Spring/Summer 1997.
4. Ronald F. Goldman, *Circumcision: The Hidden Trauma*. Boston: Vanguard, 1997.

Helga

1. Carol Lynn Mithers, *Therapy Gone Mad: The True Story of Hundreds of Patients and a Generation Betrayed*. New York: Addison-Wesley, 1994.

2. C. J. Deutsch, *Professional Psychology: Research and Practice* 16, S. 305–315, in C. J. Deutsch, *A Survey of Therapists' Personal Problems and Treatment.* 1985.

Margot and Lilka

1. Blanca Rosenberg, *To Tell at Last: Survival under False Identity, 1941–45.* Board of Trustees of the University of Illinois, 1993.

What Is Hatred?

1. Alice Miller, *Banished Knowledge.* New York: Doubleday, 1990.
2. Myron R. Sharaf, *Fury on Earth.* New York: Farrar, Straus & Giroux, 1983.
3. Alice Miller, *For Your Own Good* (New York: Farrar, Straus & Giroux, 1983); *The Untouched Key* (New York: Anchor Books, 1991); *Breaking Down the Wall of Silence* (New York: Meridian, 1997).
4. Philip J. Greven, Jr., *Spare the Child.* New York: Alfred A. Knopf, 1991.
5. Miller, *For Your Own Good.*
6. Wolfgang Sovsky, *Traktat über de Gewalt (Tractate on Violence).* Frankfurt: Fischer Verlag, 1996.
7. Daniel J. Goldhagen, *Hitler's Willing Executioners.* New York: Alfred A. Knopf, 1996.
8. Morton Schatzman, *Soul Murder: Persecution in the Family.* New York: New American Library, 1976.
9. Wilhelm G. Niederland, *The Schreber Case.* Mahwah, NJ: Lawrence Erlbaum, 1984.
10. Samuel P. Oliner and Pearl M. Oliner, *The Altruistic Personality: Rescuers of Jews in Nazi Europe.* New York: The Free Press, 1988.
11. *Le Monde,* September 6, 1996.

Postscript

1. Alice Miller, *Dein gerettetes Leben.* Frankfurt: Suhrkamp Verlag, 2007 (English version *Free From Lies* forthcoming from W. W. Norton).

ABOUT THE AUTHOR

DR. ALICE MILLER trained and practiced as a
psychoanalyst in Switzerland. Since 1980, she
has dedicated herself to writing books in
which she shares with her readers the results
of her research on childhood.

Board MTG.
Lily
Susan - - Dev. Rep. q. to me
foxtoay -
Jeanne
Joanne

Elaine Lying?
Martin -

Group -
Seslee -
Vacation - no sense of humor.
Doctor -

Tesa whispering - Jewelry up saw
Susan whispering -
& asking me
Dev. Rep.